the little Web book

By Alfred and Emily Glossbrenner

Illustrations by John Grimes

 Peachpit Press

The Little Web Book
Alfred and Emily Glossbrenner

Peachpit Press
2414 Sixth Street
Berkeley, CA 94710
800/283-9444
510/548-4393
510/548-5991 (fax)

Find us on the World Wide Web at: **http://www.peachpit.com**

Peachpit Press is a division of Addison Wesley Longman

Editor: Nolan Hester
Cover design: **TMA** Ted Mader Associates
Cover illustration: John Grimes
Interior design: David Van Ness
Copy editor: Liz Sizensky

ISBN 0-201-88367-8

9 8 7 6 5 4 3 2

Printed and bound in the United States of America

♻ Printed on recycled paper

 PRINTED WITH SOY INK

About the Authors

Alfred Glossbrenner is the author of 35 books on personal computers, online services, the Internet, and other topics. Hailed as "The Great Communicator" by the *New York Times*, he has been a freelance writer, editor, and book packager since graduating from Princeton in 1972. The best known of his noncomputer-related books are *The Art of Hitting .300* (Hawthorn, 1980) and *The Winning Hitter* (Hearst, 1984), both written with the late, great Charley Lau. The thread that unites these books with his computer titles is an uncanny knack for explaining complex subjects in a way that anyone can understand.

Emily Glossbrenner has nearly two decades' experience with computers and online communications, including nine years with the IBM Corporation as a marketing representative and marketing manager for Fortune 500 accounts. She is the coauthor of *Internet Slick Tricks* (Random House, 1994), *Making Money on the Internet* (McGraw-Hill, 1995), *Finding a Job on the Internet* (McGraw-Hill, 1995), and *The Complete Modem Handbook* (MIS:Press, 1995). In addition, she has contributed to numerous books and articles about the Internet, personal computers, and online services.

The Glossbrenners live in a 1790s farmhouse on the Delaware River in Bucks County, Pennsylvania.

Other Glossbrenner Books

The Little Online Book
by Alfred Glossbrenner

The Complete Modem Handbook
by Alfred and Emily Glossbrenner

Online Resources for Business
by Alfred Glossbrenner and John Rosenberg

Making Money on the Internet, Second Edition
by Alfred and Emily Glossbrenner

Finding a Job on the Internet
by Alfred and Emily Glossbrenner

The Information Broker's Handbook, Second Edition
by Sue Rugge and Alfred Glossbrenner

Internet 101: A College Student's Guide, Third Edition
by Alfred Glossbrenner

Internet Slick Tricks
by Alfred and Emily Glossbrenner

Table of Contents

Preface

The Internet's World Wide Web is the hottest thing to hit town since the IBM PC appeared way back in 1981. Everyone, it seems, is "cruising the Web" and "surfin' the Net," and now you can, too—quickly, easily, and with a lot of fun along the way.

That's because, unlike some books, this one won't bog you down with tons of needless "bytehead" detail. And it doesn't simply shovel 50 or 60 Web site addresses onto the page and suggest that you go visit them all.

The Little Web Book will show you what you need to know about the leading World Wide Web and Internet features and then tell you which *specific* features and locations to try.

Our recommendations are anything but random. As you will discover, there are many topic-specific chapters in this book, and each one of them contains the addresses of several sites we think anyone interested in the topic should visit.

We know because we have surveyed the field in each case, visited lots of sites, and brought you the *best!* But, of course, new sites are being added every day. That's why we've made a special effort to equip you with the tools you'll need to discover the latest sites on the Net.

The Little Web Book is divided into these parts:

Part 1, "The Web: A World of Possibilities," assumes you know absolutely nothing about going online, about the Web and the Internet and what both can do for you, or about how to get connected. The chapters here will have you up and online in a twinkling.

Part 2, "The Main Internet Features," describes the main features you'll encounter, including, of course, the World Wide Web. The chapters here will also introduce you to a kind of software called a "Web browser."

Part 3, "Hands On: How to Really *Use* The Internet!" gives you the skills you need to be a full-fledged participant in the Internet, including sending and receiving electronic mail (e-mail), downloading files, and participating in ongoing discussions with people all over the globe.

Part 4, "How and Where to Find Things on the Internet," shows you how to quickly lay your hands on whatever the Internet has to offer on any topic, no matter how obscure.

Part 5, "The World Wide Web in Your Life," begins with art and ends with travel. In alphabetical order along the way, you'll find chapters about computer help, games, humor, personal finance, and many other aspects of life as we know it—each with a Web connection!

"The Web Browser Cookbook" is the place to look for help in using your Web browser. The emphasis is on clear, step-by-step instructions for performing basic operations, including not only working with the Web but also handling e-mail and discussion groups.

The Internet Toolkit and Glossbrenner's Choice Appendix makes available on disk the files and programs we've found especially useful for getting the most out of the Internet. All of this material is available on the Net but is offered here as a convenience to our readers.

The Web: A World of Possibilities

one

The World Wide Web Will Change Your Life!

Unless you've been asleep or otherwise under heavy sedation for the last year or so, you've certainly at least heard of the World Wide Web, the Internet, and "going online."

In fact, it's been impossible to avoid encountering those terms, what with all the magazine cover stories, TV news segments, and radio programs that have been devoted to some aspect of the online world. Even the staid, gray *New York Times* has been known in recent months to carry not one but two Internet-related stories on its front page, above the fold—to say nothing of the regular clutch of online and Internet stories it runs every Monday.

Of course, being aware of a term is one thing, and having anything other than a vague idea of what it means is something else again. That's sort of the way we feel about mosh pits, triglycerides, dark matter, and the flat tax. And how could it be otherwise? We're all bombarded by so many ideas, trends, and terms that it's hard to know which ones are worth remembering.

Changing Your Life

Well, we're here to tell you that the "Web" and the "Net," as the World Wide Web and the Internet are often called, are definitely worth your time.

Yes, they've been hyped to high heaven. And yes, they've sparked more fatuous claims and addlepated predictions than you'll find on the most outrageous TV infomercial or talk show. Yet they're definitely not a flash-in-the-pan fad. The World Wide Web and the Internet are here to stay, and they truly do have the potential to change your life.

"And just how are they going to do that?" you ask. Answering that question is what this book is about. But as a quick answer, think of the World Wide Web and the Internet as *tools* that have been created for your use—tools like television, radio, and the telephone.

The Web and the Net, however, are tools with a difference, for they put *you* in charge. They put *you* in control of what you will see or hear on your computer screen. And they give *you* the power to search for and find the information (or entertainment, images, or recreational activities) you want or need.

Real-Life Examples

Sounds great in the abstract, doesn't it? But let us tell you, using examples drawn from *our* lives over the past four or five days, what the Web and the Net can really mean in your life.

It's *Your* Money!

Alfred was in the shower listening to a financial advisor on the radio. An auto mechanic wanted advice on how to invest $30,000, and the advisor suggested mutual funds. He told the caller to get the January 6, 1996, edition of the *Wall Street Journal* for its ranking of mutual funds. Pick the top five performers, send them each the same amount of money for the next three months, and repeat the process over and over to effect "dollar-cost averaging."

Assuming you've got some money to invest, what do you do if you don't subscribe to the *Wall Street Journal*, or if your personal copy has long since been hauled away for recycling?

You could go to the library, of course. But you could also go online and get the *same* information—without ever leaving home or toweling

your hair dry! The Lipper Mutual
Fund Scorecard is but one of
many similar features you will find
at the *Wall Street Journal*'s Web
address, **http://update.wsj.com**.
(Web addresses are explained later.
For now, just think of them as
words you type into your computer
to tell it to take you to a particular
location.)

Mutual fund rankings online.

Public Issues and Public TV

The next day, Emily was doing
some interior painting, demon-
strating her world-class talent at "cutting in" crown molding and chair
rails. The TV was tuned to CNN as Jack Kemp and his Tax Reform
Commission presented their report. Speaker Gingrich made some comment about making the report available on the World Wide Web.

Unless you're a political junkie or are having trouble getting to
sleep at night, you're not likely to read commission reports of any kind.
What's of interest about this story is the fact that at least four publishers turned down a proposal to publish the Tax Reform Commission
report as a book.

So what did the commission
do? It "published" the report itself
on the Internet by placing copies
on both the Thomas Legislative
Information Web site (see Chapter
28 for more on Thomas) and a site
called "Town Hall" at
http://www.townhall.com.

Think about what this means:
Regardless of your views (left,
right, or anarchist), regardless of
your facts or arguments, you and
everyone else can "publish" on the

Town Hall on the World Wide Web.

World Wide Web and the Internet. If you've got something to say, you are no longer at the mercy of traditional paper-and-ink publishers, distribution systems, editors, or anything else.

Generally, any public document of interest can be found online and downloaded to your computer for printing or saving to disk. But, while many public documents are boring, public TV is not. So you will be glad to hear that many PBS TV and radio stations are already on the World Wide Web.

The big PBS station in our area is WHYY in Philadelphia. So we logged on to **http://www.whyy.org**, just as the announcer suggested we do, and found, among other things, the daily schedule for the month of January. Click on a day of the month, and you will see a listing of public TV programs.

Netscape - [January on TV12!]

File Edit View Go Bookmarks Options Directory Window Help

Location: http://www.whyy.org/TV12Schedule.html

Here are the daily schedules for TV12. Click on any date to see what's on that day.

January 1996

SUNDAY	MONDAY	TUESDAY	WEDNESDAY	THURSDAY	FRIDAY	SATURDAY
	1	2	3	4	5	6
7	8	9	10	11	12	13
14	15	16	17	18	19	20
21	22	23	24	25	26	27
28	29	30	31			

Document Done

Click on a day.

Homework and Hitchhiking

We recently spent an afternoon at our local library. The reference librarian was overburdened, so when a 15-year-old asked for help finding magazine articles for a school report about the dangers of hitchhiking, we offered to show the kid how to use the Wilsonline CD-ROM.

Netscape - [TV12 schedule - January 1996]

File Edit View Go Bookmarks Options Directory Window Help

Location: http://whyy.org/TV4Jan96.html#30

6:00 THE NEWSHOUR WITH JIM LEHRER
7:00 NIGHTLY BUSINESS REPORT
7:30 AS TIME GOES BY
8:00 NOVA "B-29: Frozen in Time" An expedition to the Humboldt Glacier in Greenland, where in 1947 a B-29 was ditched and has since remained untouched for over 45 years. [CC]
9:00 BRITISH RAIL JOURNEYS "Southwest: Exeter to Penzance" Vintage rail cars and modern high speed railways provide a first class tour of the British countryside.
10:00 SO YOU WANT TO BUY A PRESIDENT? (Frontline) An estimated $300 million will flow into the coffers of the 1996 presidential candidate's campaign funds. What do big donors expect for their contributions? [CC]
11:00 GREAT CRIMES AND TRIALS OF THE 20TH CENTURY This special series documents the world's most notorious killers. "The Manson Family Murders" turns the spotlight on the horrific exploits of Charles Manson and his followers.
12:00 CHARLIE ROSE
1:00 SIGN-OFF

JANUARY 31 Wednesday
6:30 BLOOMBERG BUSINESS NEWS
7:00 SESAME STREET

Document Done

Public TV program listings on the Web.

the kid how to use the Wilsonline CD-ROM.

Three articles about hitchhiking showed up. Unfortunately, they were all about the joys and adventures of this activity, not the dangers. We had to leave, but suggested that the student search on the word "abduction."

We have no idea how things turned out, but the question rankled. If we were her parents, what would we do? So we searched the World Wide Web on the terms "abduction" and "children" and "safety." Bingo! No fewer than 82 places to look turned up, any one of which we could reach by simply clicking the mouse button.

These included the StreetSmart home page (**http://www.cache.net/ streetsmart**), with its offers of affordably priced videotape training materials, and a site called SAFE-T-CHILD Online (**http://yellodino. safe-t-child.com**). One truly neat feature of SAFE-T-CHILD is a five-minute quiz that you and your child can take to rate his or her "street smarts."

Cheeseheads Can Save Your Life!

Finally, time out for a bit of fun. Emily's brother loves funny hats and headgear. So when we heard Michael Feldman on the radio program

Whad'ya Know talk about the private-plane pilot who saved his life by donning a foam "cheese-head" just before crashing, we just had to check the Net. Certainly there was no guarantee that this company would be on the Net. But putting up a Web site has become so cheap and so many companies are doing it, that it was well worth looking.

Cheeseheads and more online!

Sure enough, we found a site maintained by Foamation, the company that created the cheese-head wedge, cowboy hat, clip-on tie, earrings, and other accessories (**http://www.arcfile.com/chezhead.html**). Needless to say, Emily's brother got a Foamation cheesehead hat for Christmas!

Enriching Your Life

These are all real-life examples. We didn't invent anything to make it play better in this book. The Internet and the World Wide Web have simply become a normal part of our lives. The same may happen to you.

When you hear a word you don't know, you reach for *Webster's Collegiate Dictionary*. When you want to know what's on tonight, you root around until you find *TV Guide*. When you want to know about anything else—art, entertainment, books, government, jobs, careers, medicine, or a kid's homework assignment—you can check the Net and the Web!

The Internet as a whole, and the World Wide Web in particular, have become tools that empower us and enrich our lives. Very little effort is required. All you need is some run-of-the-mill computer equipment and the kind of guidance you'll find in the pages of this book.

String along with us. We'll show you how easy it is to change and enrich your life by "going online"—just as we've showed literally hundreds of thousands of others. It's easy. It's cheap. It's fun. And it has the firepower of a ton of dynamite!

(E-MAIL) *for* (PENNIES)

(LIVELY DISCUSSION)

(INFORMATION) *From* (SOUP) *To* (NUTS)

What *Is* the World Wide Web Anyhow?

*At this point, you know that the World Wide Web and the
Internet have at least the potential to enhance your life.
But before we go any further, we'd better take just a moment
to get a clearer idea of what we're dealing with here.*

The Future, Back Then

There are just two main points to hold onto. First, the Internet is really
nothing more than the collection of wires, switches, and software that
makes it possible for computers all over the world to "talk" to each
other. It's like the whole physical infrastructure used to bring TV or
radio signals to your home set.

But what good are signals if they aren't organized into a form that
you can use? You don't want to get radio signals on your TV, or CB signals on your AM/FM tuner, after all.

That's where the second point comes in. The World Wide Web is
like the television portion of the electromagnetic spectrum. As you
might expect, within this spectrum there are many, many "channels"
from which to choose—thousands and thousands of channels in fact,
each carrying its own special "show."

But, while the World Wide Web may be the most popular portion
of the spectrum right now, it is only part of what's available. As we'll
see later, there are all kinds of other Internet features that have no
more to do with the World Wide Web than cellular phones have to do
with AM/FM radio.

What James Bond Never Knew

But first we'll lay in a little background about the Internet itself. You
can use this information to impress people at cocktail parties. But you
will also find that what we're about to tell you removes a lot of the mystery and makes the Net much more understandable.

The story begins 20 to 30 years ago, a time when only big companies and big government agencies could afford computers, which is to
say, the gigantic, water-cooled "big iron" beasts called "mainframes."

You know, like the computer Spencer Tracy installed to automate Katharine Hepburn's research department in the 1957 movie *Desk Set*. (Worth renting if you've never seen it.)

Typically, a company would buy or lease a mainframe and install it in its headquarters location. People at the company's branch offices would communicate with the mainframe using "dumb terminals." These were basically a keyboard and a video screen connected to the mainframe by a telephone line.

Think of the hub and spokes of a wagon wheel. The mainframe is at the center of the hub. The spokes are the phone lines that terminate in a dumb terminal at each end. Under this arrangement, the only way the various terminals can communicate with each other is by going through the hub.

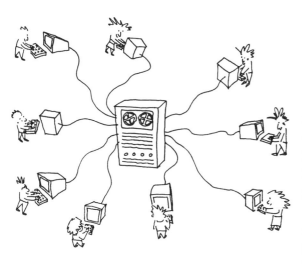

So what happens if there's a massive power failure that shuts down the mainframe hub? Or a massive nuclear strike that wipes out the hub completely? What happens if the one phone line leading from Cleveland to the hub is severed?

Hey, wait a minute . . . "a massive nuclear strike?" What is this? Isn't the Cold War a relic of history?

Quite right. But 25 years ago, the Cold War and the possibility of a nuclear strike were very much on people's minds. Or at least on the minds of people at the Pentagon who are paid to think the unthinkable.

It turns out that the traditional hub-and-spoke model is extremely vulnerable. You can bury the "hub" computer beneath a blast-hardened mountain, but you can't possibly protect all your spokes. (Remember, there's only one phone line connecting Cleveland to the hub. Sever it, and there is no longer any way to communicate with that city.)

The Network Concept

This fact became clear to the deep thinkers at the Pentagon in the 1960s. So the Advanced Research Projects Agency (ARPA) of the Department of Defense hired the firm of Bolt, Beranek, and Newman (BBN) to solve the problem. What BBN came up with eventually changed the world. It was called the ARPANET, but in simple terms, it was a computer network, or, in technical terms, a "packet-switching network."

In this network, there is no single path between Point A and Point B. Thanks to "alternative routing," there are thousands of paths a given message can take to reach its destination. The essential concept is as simple as the children's chant, "If Paula can't do it, Jonathan can, and if Jonathan can't do it, Sarah can, and if Sarah can't do it . . ." and so on.

Everything depends on deploying thousands of computers all over the country, linking them together with multiple phone lines, and having them run special software that turns each machine into an intelligent switch.

The End (and the Beginning) of an Era

That's really all most people need to know about the physical structure of the Internet. Sure, some connections are much faster than others, and yes, the operating speeds of the computers on the Net vary greatly. But all we need to know is that we can type in the address of a computer somewhere, and the Net will connect us to it.

Okay, so who created all the features available on the Net today? Somebody had to do it. After all, if no feature is running on the distant computer, why bother to connect? Why turn on the TV if there's no programming?

Good questions, all. The answer is that most Internet features were created by the Net's original users. You see, the Department of Defense used the ARPANET to connect military bases, defense contractors, and universities that were doing defense-related research. And that's all.

For the next 21 years, the only way to gain access to the Net was to be a member of one of these groups. Only in January of 1990, after the Cold War was well and truly over, was the public at large allowed in. And, as you might imagine, what we of the unwashed masses found was a thriving, deeply engrained culture that, frankly, wasn't too happy to see our bright shining faces. (Never mind that our tax dollars built this nifty little sandbox in the first place.)

Of course, the ARPANET was only the beginning. Over time, numerous other organizations, institutions, and the like developed similar networks of their own. And then, of course, the networks began to link up. That's why you will often hear the Internet called the "network of networks."

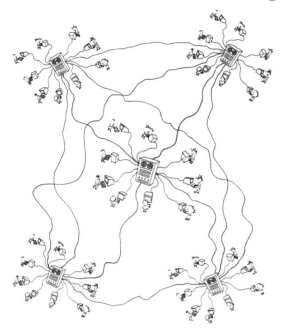

THE INTERNET: A NETWORK OF NETWORKS

A Word About Non-Web Features

Surprising as it may seem, the World Wide Web is really the newest Internet feature. And, while the Web is certainly the most exciting feature, you'll be missing out on a lot if the Web is all you know. True story: We were doing a radio interview when someone called in and asked if there was anything else to the Internet beyond the World Wide Web.

It was a perfect leading question, and the fact that someone would ask it was perfectly understandable. The truth is that the Internet also makes it possible for you to send and receive "electronic mail" or "e-mail." That means that you can communicate with virtually anyone on the planet who has an Internet account or who subscribes to systems like America Online, CompuServe, Prodigy, Delphi, MCI Mail, and the like.

Think about this: You can send a message anywhere in the world at a cost of a few pennies, if that, and the message will be there in *seconds*! No need to worry about postage or writing on special onion-skin paper to keep the weight down.

Discussions of *Everything*

E-mail is personal, limited to people you know. So let's broaden the scope. Pick a topic, any topic, and you can read what people have to say about it on the Internet. The last time we checked, there were over 15,000 topics being discussed in Internet "newsgroups."

Topics range from the sublime to the ridiculous, from the mundane to the obscene. You will find discussions devoted to just about any computer hardware or software topic you can imagine. That figures, given the Internet's "bytehead" origins. But you will also find discussions devoted to any kind of music played anywhere in the world, past or present, and almost every leading artist or band. And you will find discussions of topics such as these:

- *A Prairie Home Companion*
- Arthritis and related disorders
- Baseball cards and memorabilia
- Bird-watching
- Chess, backgammon, Chinese checkers, bridge, etc.
- Coffee: making and drinking
- Computer science education
- Cookbooks and recipes
- Family vacations
- Formula One motor racing
- Gardens, orchards, and hybridizing
- High school marching bands
- Humor and joke collections
- Items wanted and items for sale
- J. R. R. Tolkien
- Japanese comic fanzines
- Physical fitness, exercise, bodybuilding, etc.
- Quilting
- Soap operas
- Wines

"Real" Information

Okay, so maybe you don't count what you find in newsgroups as "real" information. Fair enough. But how about official weather reports, scholarly papers, access to the Library of Congress, the transcripts of presidential speeches, every Supreme Court decision, and tons of material from agencies of the federal government?

How about Project Gutenberg and the Online Book Initiative, two organizations that have made available hundreds of classic works of literature in electronic form free of charge? Now you can easily scan, say, the full text of *Moby Dick* for every occurrence of the word "orphan." (This is a real example—we have a friend who did her master's thesis on orphan imagery in *Moby Dick*.)

How the Web Came to Be

You will find much more about how to take advantage of non-Web features later in this book. But now we need to complete the story, or at least the story so far.

The Internet was built. The physical connections were established. And over the decades, various features (like e-mail, newsgroups, and "FTP" file transfers) were created and offered by Net users. Some were accepted by the community. Some were not. But over time, a general set of familiar Internet features evolved.

That's how things were done. So in March 1989, when Tim Berners-Lee of the European Lab for Particle Physics (known as CERN) proposed a way of using the Internet to make research information more easily available to the scientific community, he was operating within long-established norms—which is to say, run it up the Net flagpole and see if anyone salutes.

Basically, Berners-Lee suggested that scientists look at the Internet as a huge, "we never close" library when preparing their papers. As every college student knows, scholarly articles are filled with cross-references and footnotes. If you want to follow up on these sources, you must hunt them down yourself, using traditional library resources. What Berners-Lee said was, in effect, "Hey, let's make all those cross-references 'clickable!' Click on a cross-referenced book, article, or paper, and it instantly appears on your screen, thanks to the Internet."

That's how the World Wide Web began, only it wasn't really "clickable" in the beginning. The "hypertext links" that would deliver a copy of a footnoted article to your terminal screen were all text.

Enter Mosaic and Then Netscape

The Berners-Lee concept of the World Wide Web began to take hold. But it didn't take off until the National Center for Supercomputing Applications (NCSA) began a project to create a *graphical* user interface for the Web. That happened in 1993 to 1994, and the program was called "Mosaic."

Mosaic not only made it possible for you to click your way through the Web with your mouse, but it also allowed you to view documents with images and to transfer video and sound data over the Internet. In essence, Tim Berners-Lee established the idea of hypertext links, now called "hot links," and Mosaic added a graphical, Windows/Macintosh-style interface.

The result was a means of using the Internet's World Wide Web to click from one location to another, with everything looking like a page from a slick magazine, complete with different type styles, color illustrations, and hot links to still other pages.

The team that created Mosaic broke away to establish a separate company. They named the new entity Netscape Communications, and they called their "Web browser" software product Netscape Navigator. But today, everyone calls the program "Netscape."

Netscape has been tearing up the track ever since, in both the software market and the stock market. And that's where we are today. In the next chapter, we'll show you how to equip yourself for life in this wonderful new universe.

Keys to the Kingdom: Modems and Software

3

WHAT TO LOOK FOR IN A MODEM:

- SPEED ("BAUD" RATE)
  - 14,400 BPS (BITS/SEC.) AT LEAST
  - 28,800 BPS - PREFERRED
- PRICE: $100.-$300. ±
- INTERNAL V. EXTERNAL?
- RELIABILITY; TECH SUPPORT

Tapping into the Internet has never been simpler. All you need is a computer, a device called a "modem," a communications software package, and, of course, a telephone. (You also need an account on a system that offers Internet access, but we'll cover that topic in the next chapter.)

It's important to point out that *any* computer will do. Just because you use an old IBM AT-level "286" or a Mac Classic doesn't mean you can't get on the Net. You can. The graphic images you'll encounter may take a lot longer to appear on your screen if you're using an older, slower computer, but appear they will.

At some point, you may want to buy a more powerful computer with a bigger, faster hard disk drive and all the multimedia bells and whistles. But there's no need to do so just to use the Internet and the World Wide Web.

Next, there's the matter of the modem. You need a modem because phone lines are designed to carry sound. Computers, in contrast, communicate using voltage pulses. It is the modem's job to convert voltage pulses into sound and vice versa. Naturally, there's a lot more to it than this. We're dealing with computers, after all. But that's the essence of the thing.

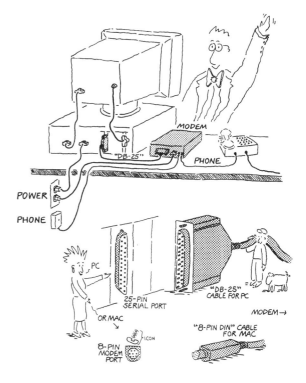

How to Buy a Modem

It's possible that you may already have a modem in your computer and not know it. Look at the back of the machine and see if there is any place where you can plug in a modular phone cord. If there is, you almost certainly have an internal modem. Check the literature that came with your computer to find out for sure.

If you've got to buy a modem, you need remember only one sentence: *Buy an external 28.8/V.34 data/fax modem.* Expect to pay about $170 (or less) from a computer mail-order company. Leading modem makers include Zoom, Supra, Cardinal, Hayes, US Robotics, and Boca Research. Just make sure that you also get the cable needed to connect the modem to your computer. The cost for the cable will be about $5.

And the Reasons Why

That's really all you absolutely need to know about buying a modem, unless you want to communicate using a laptop computer when you're on the road. In that case, you will want one of those credit card-size PC Card modems. They're expensive, but they are also very light.

There is no difference in performance between internal and external modems. Given a choice, the only reason for considering an internal modem is if your computer was manufactured prior to 1993, as explained in the sidebar "Have You Checked Your UART?"

The reason we like external modems is that you can easily turn them off to break a connection when you're "hung up" and because they have little lights that tell you what's going on, like when information is coming in or going out. There's also the fact that an external modem can be used with *any* kind of computer.

The designation "28.8/V.34" refers to a modem's speed, and at this writing, that is the fastest modem speed available. The next level down is 14.4/V.17, but that's really too slow to use the Web and the Net with comfort. In other words, pay a little more to get a 28.8/V.34.

As for fax capability, virtually every modem on the market lets you send and receive faxes on your computer. And yes, they come with the fax software you need to do it.

Have You Checked Your UART?

This does not apply to Macintosh computers. But if your non-Macintosh ("Wintel") computer was manufactured as late as 1993, it may have difficulty working effectively with today's high-speed (28.8/V.34) modems. The bottleneck lies with a little chip called a UART. That's short for Universal Asynchronous Receiver/Transmitter. This is the chip that is at the heart of your computer's communications port or "serial card."

Older chips can handle a top speed of 9.6, far less than a speed of 28.8. So how can you find out what kind of UART you've got? The answer is to run the Microsoft Diagnostics program that comes with MS-DOS 6 and above. Hit "C" for "Com Port" and see what the program has to say.

The screen that will then appear will include an item labeled "UART Chip Used." If the chip number is "8250," you have an old, slow UART. What you want is a chip with a number beginning with "165" or higher, like "16550AF."

In general, the higher the chip number, the better. Computer dealers can sell you a high-speed serial card for about $25. But if you're a real speed fan, consider a souped-up card like the Lava-650 card for Windows users. Built around the zippy new 16650 UART and equipped with a 32-byte buffer, this item has a list price of $59.95. For more information, contact Lava Computer Manufacturing at 416-674-5942.

The alternative to buying a high-speed serial card and an external modem is to buy an internal 28.8 modem, since you can be sure that such modems will contain a UART able to operate at that speed.

A Bit More on Modem Speed

You may be wondering just what is measured when comparing modem speeds. What does "28.8" refer to in physical terms? The answer is that modem speeds are measured in "bits per second (bps)," as in a speed of 28,800 bits per second. Or they are measured in "kilobits—one thousand bits—per second (Kbps)," as in 28.8 kilobits per second. (Bits, of course, are the binary digits—the 1s and 0s—all computers use to communicate.)

The V.34 designation is pronounced "vee dot thirty-four." It refers to the international standard that sets forth exactly which techniques modems will use to communicate at a speed of 28.8 kilobits per second. The standard was worked out by a unit of the United Nations.

What About Software?

Finally, there is the generally good news about software. Your modem will almost certainly come with a basic online communications program and a fax program. It may even include a program that lets you turn your computer into a voice mail system!

But these programs are usually "lite" versions of commercial products. Like the terminal programs built into Windows and Macintosh System 7, they are adequate, but there is little point in spending much time learning how to use them.

You will be much better off if you allow CompuServe, Prodigy, America Online, or some other commercial service to *give* you the software you need to access their systems, browse the World Wide Web, and work with the Internet.

Now let's see about getting you connected!

Necessary Connections
for Beginners

4

There are lots of ways to get connected to the Internet. If you work for a defense contractor or other big company, are in the military, or attend college, gaining access may be a simple matter of asking the people who manage your organization's computers and local area networks.

Don't be surprised, however, if the company policy is to restrict Internet access. Some firms see the Internet as a drain on productivity that will make the solitaire game built into Windows pale by comparison. And they're probably right!

On the consumer side, there are really two main choices. You can gain access to the Net via a mass-market consumer system like Compu-Serve, Prodigy, America Online, Microsoft Network, or a similar system. Or you can get an account with an Internet Service Provider (ISP).

The main difference is this: A mass-market consumer system offers help and customer support, plus exclusive non-Internet features of its own. Internet Service Providers, in contrast, typically give you the necessary software and a phone number to dial to get connected, and that's it. Don't expect much in the way of customer support or hand-holding from an ISP.

On the other hand, mass-market consumer systems charge about $10 a month for five hours of connect time, with each additional hour billed at about $3. Internet Service Providers, in contrast, usually charge $15 to $20 a month for *unlimited* Internet access.

If You're a Newbie

If you are indeed a "newbie"—someone who is just getting started with the online world and with the Internet—you simply cannot expect to be able to plunge into the deep end of the pool the first time out. That's why we strongly recommend starting with one of the Big Three consumer systems: America Online, CompuServe, or Prodigy. Microsoft Network may be a worthy choice as well, but it simply does not have the experience the Big Three have in guiding new users into the online world.

Regardless of the system you choose, you can cancel at any time, so you can't go too far wrong. It is the mass-market consumer systems that we'll look at here. Once you've gained some experience, you may want to consider making an Internet Service Provider your main access point. We will consider this option in the *next* chapter.

Why Start with a Consumer System?

America Online, CompuServe, and Prodigy are known as the Big Three because they have more subscribers than any of their competitors. Millions more, in fact. Each was established years ago, long before the craze for the Web and the Internet hit.

All three will give you the software you need, and they'll throw in a free five- or ten-hour trial period, after which you can cancel and not owe them a dime. You can get one of these subscription offers by dialing a toll-free number, but you probably won't have to.

Any more, you'll find disks and offers from America Online, CompuServe, and Prodigy in your mail, bound into magazines, in the box your modem came in, and possibly even pre-loaded onto your new computer. So, basically, you can sample these systems risk-free, and, of course, you can cancel your subscription at any time.

The Magic of Special Interest Groups and Forums

As we've said, the mass-market consumer systems emphasize customer hand-holding and support. You may have to wend your way through a voice-mail maze and then spend a considerable amount of time waiting to talk to a real human being, but at least the Big Three offer round-the-clock, toll-free customer support lines.

Even more important, in our opinion, is the fact that each consumer system has one or more Internet-oriented "Forum" or "Special Interest Group (SIG)." If you've never been online before, you should know that these features are like online clubhouses.

There are "rooms" where you can chat in real time with other members. There is a message board where you can post questions—and search for answers. And there are libraries that contain helpful files and programs that you can download to your own computer.

Special Interest Groups and Forums are usually managed by a "system operator" or "sysop" (pronounced "sis-op") and one or more assistants. It is their responsibility to see that things are kept in good order, that your questions are answered promptly, that the files in the library are fresh, and so on.

There is no extra charge for using these features. The sysops are there to take care of you, and most do a splendid job.

A Quick Example

Nothing like this exists on the Internet or the World Wide Web. Or to put it more accurately, what does exist is but a pale imitation of what you'll find on a consumer system. There are indeed "newsgroups" on the Net for posting messages and replies. While some have "moderators," there are no sysops to see that your questions are answered.

For example, you might post a question about where to get a program that will let you view graphic images. Some good-hearted soul may respond with detailed, step-by-step instructions, but you can't count on it. And you may have to wait a week or more for such a reply.

On one of the Big Three systems, in contrast, you can go to an Internet or Web Forum or Special Interest Group and post your question. If no one responds within several hours, there's a good chance that the sysop will do so personally. He or she will say something like, "What you need is a program like Graphic Workshop. You'll find a copy in this Forum in Library 12. The file to download is GWS.ZIP. Let me know if you have any questions."

Order Out of Chaos

Finally, there is the value that the Big Three consumer systems add by organizing and packaging information and features. This is a very, very important point, though it may be a while before you grasp the significance of the fact.

More than likely, you'll have to "drink from the firehose" of information on the Internet and the World Wide Web before you can appreciate the filtering, editing, and information-packaging skills the Big Three have been perfecting for years. In our opinion, many Internet users will eventually conclude that services like these are well worth paying for.

And Our Recommendation Is . . .

Thus, when you are a complete novice, there is no question about the best approach: Start with one of the Big Three! But which one? Well, as you know, you can try each system for free, and if you have the time, you probably should do so.

Our personal recommendation for newbies, however, is America Online. No other system so seamlessly integrates the Web and the Net into its own service. CompuServe and Prodigy have a great deal to offer, but they are still playing catch-up in this regard.

Of course, things have been moving quite fast in

America Online is more than just a pretty face. It has tightly integrated the Internet with its main system.

this field in recent years. The market is consolidating as second- and third-tier systems are either sold, merged, or discontinued. Important developments are on the horizon.Still, if you're a newbie, you can't go far wrong with one of the current Big Three in general and with America Online in particular.

Resources

America Online (AOL)
800-827-6364

CompuServe Information Service (CIS)
800-848-8199

Prodigy Information Services
800-776-3449

Microsoft Network (MSN)
800-386-5550

Advanced Connections, Once You're Hooked

5

This chapter assumes that you have either been using the Internet and the World Wide Web for several months via one of the Big Three or another online service, or that you have been using computers long enough that fending for yourself, with very little in the way of customer support, doesn't bother you.

Now, flash back to the last time you were online surfing the World Wide Web via America Online, CompuServe, or Prodigy. You're checking out the Cool Site of the Day, hotlinking hither and yon, and generally having a ball. Then you happen to glance at the clock.

Uh-oh. You've got to be kidding! Could I possibly have been online for three whole hours? Good grief, how much have I spent? Lemme see, three hours at $2.95 each comes to $8.85. Yikes!

That's like blowing the entire week's online budget in a single evening. And it's so very easy to do, almost without noticing it. Before long you find that your monthly online charges are within hailing distance of your car payment.

When to Switch to an Internet Service Provider

The Big Three charge $9.95 a month for five hours of access and $2.95 an hour after that. Most Internet Service Providers (ISPs), in contrast, charge about $20 for a nearly unlimited number of connect-time hours. So the question is: How many hours of connect time will $20 get you on one of the Big Three? The answer is about 8.5 hours.

If you're currently spending *more* than 8.5 hours a month tapping the Net via one of the Big Three, it may be time to switch to an ISP. In fact, switching sounds like a no-brainer, doesn't it?

Yes, it does—until you realize how chaotic the ISP marketplace is and consider what you can and cannot expect to get for your monthly fee. This chapter will help guide you through the minefields.

Chaos in the Marketplace, Again

There are hundreds, if not thousands, of Internet Service Providers nationwide. They range from big, well-financed companies like AT&T and MCI to individuals with about $10,000 to invest in their long-held dream of having their own small, mom-and-pop-style business.

Their prices and policies vary all over the lot. But the main issues are connect-time cost, freedom of choice in the software you can use to access the Net, and the depth and availability of customer service.

Connect-Time Cost

An ISP can cut your Internet usage costs in two ways. First, it offers a lower connect-time rate. Unless you live far from a major city, there's a good chance that you can find an ISP that you can access via a local call and that offers a nearly unlimited number of hours of connect time for about $20 a month. You will find many pricing variations, but that is the standard by which you should measure all ISPs.

Second, almost all ISPs offer 28.8 Kbps connections. The Big Three, in contrast, offer only a limited number of "high-speed" 28.8 numbers. Most are at 14.4 Kbps or slower. That may have changed by the time you read this. But an ISP can offer you a 28.8 Kbps connection *today*, thus cutting in half the time required to perform similar tasks on one of the Big Three.

On the other hand, it must be noted that the Big Three have not remained idle. At this writing, for example, CompuServe has just announced SpryNet, a completely separate service that will give you unlimited access to the Internet for $19.95 a month. The advantage: As part of CompuServe, SpryNet has local access phone numbers all over the world.

The disadvantages: Judging from the experience of CompuServe users, the telephone customer support for SpryNet is not likely to be very good. You may or may not have toll-free access to a 28.8 Kbps node. And then there is the matter of "censorship." CompuServe has affirmed that, at least for the time being, users of SpryNet will not be permitted to access newsgroups covering topics that may be objectionable to some people in some countries around the world. Your local ISP does not labor under such restrictions.

Software Flexibility

To someone who has really gotten into the Internet, the issue of which software he or she can use is crucial. If you're into woodworking, cooking, gardening, or another special activity, you know that once you've had some experience and really know what you're doing, you begin to get rather picky about your tools. The same is true with the Internet.

Consider e-mail: To send and receive Internet e-mail on the Big Three, you must use the e-mail module each of these systems offers. You have no choice in the matter. But if you have an ISP connection, you can use an Internet-compatible electronic mail program like Eudora or Pegasus, or some other shareware, public domain, or commercial package that offers you features you won't find among the Big Three.

For example, Eudora (available for Windows and Mac), makes it easy for you to prepare a reply to an e-mail message while you're offline. That's good, because it means you're not racking up connect-time charges as you compose your reply. You can include tagged lines from an original message, so the recipient knows what you are commenting on or referring to in your response. You can then sign on to your ISP, and Eudora will automatically transmit your replies.

Programs like Eudora and Pegasus also make it very easy to send graphic images, .ZIP and .EXE files, and other binary files as Internet e-mail "attachments." In technical terms, they automatically convert and reconvert binary files into the plain ASCII text that any computer system can handle. You don't need to know the details at this point, but that can be a big time-saver.

The Browser of Your Choice

And we haven't even mentioned the selection of World Wide Web "browser" programs you can use with most ISPs. As we will see later, browser programs like Netscape Navigator, Mosaic, and others are the hottest, fastest-developing areas of the Internet. In this environment, you want to be able to easily use any browser you please to tap the Web and the Net.

We should emphasize the word "easily." For, while it is technically possible to use *any* Web browser with CompuServe, America Online, or Prodigy, getting things set up correctly isn't always easy. As mass-market systems, the Big Three want everyone to do things their way.

ISPs have no such desires. Why? Because most Internet Service Providers figure they're in the business of offering you a connection to the Internet and little else. Most will indeed provide you with the suite of programs you'll need to surf the Web and tap other Net features. But after that, you're pretty much on your own.

Customer Support Is Expensive

After all, customer support is *expensive*. So, in general, if you assume that you will receive nothing in the way of customer support from an ISP, you definitely won't be disappointed. (What do you expect for $20 a month and unlimited 28.8 Kbps Net access, anyway?)

Now that you have a pretty good idea of your options—Big Three or ISP—we're ready to put it all together. That's what we'll do in the next chapter as we summarize the steps to follow to get connected.

Summing Up: The Steps to Follow to Get on the Net

6

Chapter 4 told you about using one of the Big Three systems to get onto the Internet and the World Wide Web. Chapter 5 introduced you to the ISP (Internet Service Provider) alternative.

Now we must add a third alternative: Flat-fee, ISP-style Internet connections offered by the Big Three and other long-established consumer online systems. In a word: The big boys have begun to muscle their way into the business of providing a simple Internet connection.

AT&T's WorldNet

We can begin with the biggest boy of all: AT&T. Early in 1996, the telephone giant startled the entire online industry by announcing that it would provide every customer five hours of free Internet access via its WorldNet service each month for a year. Additional time is billed at

$2.50 an hour. The company also announced a subscription option offering unlimited Internet access for $19.95 a month.

WorldNet customers receive Netscape Navigator software free of charge and have access to round-the-clock customer service. Access is available via over 200 dial-up numbers nationwide, which means that people in over 80 percent of the country can log on by making a local phone call.

At this writing, AT&T has over 80 million residential customers and 10 million business customers, according to the *New York Times*. Of these 90 million customers, some 20 million are believed to own personal computers and modems. As the actor Edward Herrmann says in that car commercial, "This changes everything."

Or not. It is impossible to predict what the AT&T WorldNet program will mean to the Internet industry. But it does guarantee that things will be very interesting. It also means that the prices charged by competing companies may have changed as you read this.

Global Network Navigator and SpryNet

America Online has introduced its Global Network Navigator (GNN) service. Totally separate from the main AOL system, GNN costs $14.95 a month for 20 hours of Net/Web access, with additional hours being billed at $1.95. Customer service and 20 megabytes of online storage are also part of the package. (For more information, point your Web browser at **http://www.gnn.com**, if you are already on the Net.)

Not to be outdone, CompuServe offers its Internet-only SpryNet service at a cost of $9.95 a month for seven hours, with additional hours billed at $1.95. The company has also announced a service code-named WOW!. The system isn't scheduled to become available until after this book has gone to press—but WOW! will be a graphical system aimed at brand new users, and it will offer subscribers access to at least some CompuServe forums.

Rupert Murdoch—owner of the Fox TV network, *TV Guide*, and many other properties—has announced that he will re-focus his Delphi Internet Services to concentrate more on providing Net access.

Microsoft has said that it will do the same with its Microsoft Network (MSN). And Prodigy, as well as every other current consumer-oriented online system, is considering similar moves.

What About Netcom, PSINet, and Other "National" ISPs?

In essence, the big, national consumer online systems, those that have long boasted of unique, proprietary content, have decided that if you "can't beat 'em, join 'em." They have concluded that the popularity of the Internet shouldn't be seen as a threat but as an opportunity.

We bring this up because the entry of AT&T and of the leading consumer online systems probably spells the re-structuring of companies that might be called "national Internet Service Providers." You will hear about these firms. They include companies like Netcom, PSINet, and EarthLink, and their goal has been to offer Internet access via a local phone call nationwide.

Back in the days when the only way you could log onto the Net was by dialing into your local ISP—even if you happened to be a thousand miles away at the time—a "national ISP" with lots of dial-up nodes around the country made sense. But now that the AT&T and the Big Three have entered the field, it isn't at all clear why anyone would want to subscribe to a national ISP.

Nor is it clear how a Netcom, which reportedly reached the 200,000 subscriber mark in the fall of 1995, is going to compete with an America Online (5 million subscribers) or a CompuServe (4.3 million subscribers). Or even a Prodigy (1.4 million subscribers).

In our opinion, the way small national (or even local) Internet service providers can survive is by offering superb customer service. This is something many have not done in the past. And it is something that will be increasingly difficult for the big boys to do in the future.

Resources

Netcom Online Communication Services Inc.
800-501-8649
http://www.netcom.com

PSINet
800-453-7473
http://www.psi.net

EarthLink Network, Inc.
800-876-3151
http://www.earthlink.net

SpryNet
800-777-9638
http://www.sprynet.com

Delphi Internet Systems
800-695-4005
http://www.delphi.com

① YOU ARE HERE   ② GET MODEM   ③ GET FREE TRIAL ON AOL OR OTHER (SEE APPENDIX)   ④ EXPLORE

If You're a Newbie, Go with AOL

As you know from Chapter 4, if you're a complete novice, we recommend starting with America Online. If you don't have one or more AOL "ten free hours" subscription disks lying around, call them up and request one. The number is 800-827-6364.

Why AOL? Because AOL's software, software installation procedure, customer support (both on the phone and online) and the America Online service itself, are excellent. They are ideally suited for a new online user and a new Internet user. They are well worth $9.95 a month for five hours and $2.95 per hour thereafter.

What About Prodigy?

As you read this, things will surely have changed. There is every possibility that Prodigy will have come up to AOL's standards, or it may be that CompuServe's WOW! service will be so user-friendly that it will have just taken off.

As the smallest of the Big Three, Prodigy may end up getting absorbed by some other system. But in the "credit where it's due" depart-

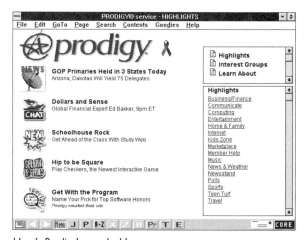

Here's Prodigy's new look!

ment we'd like to say that we have always found Prodigy to have the best real, live human telephone support in the business.

And Prodigy has recently given itself a complete facelift. When you sign onto the system today, you see screens that remind you of the World Wide Web. On the "new" Prodigy, the graphics and fonts are crisp and clear and the advertisements, which most Prodigy screens have always carried are smaller, more discrete, and more like what you are likely to encounter at a "sponsored" Web site.

What About CompuServe?

As for the CompuServe Information Service, you should know that CIS has long been our favorite of the Big Three consumer systems. The depth and breadth of information offered by CompuServe has no rival in AOL or Prodigy.

Trouble is, CompuServe is a text-based service in a graphical world. To compensate, CIS offers Windows and Macintosh programs that wrap a graphical front-end around things. It has also begun transmitting special graphic images the first time you visit a particular feature. These are stored on disk and thus appear much faster the next time you visit a feature. But, while these images further improve the way the screen looks, it is still impossible to disguise the fact that CIS is a text-based system.

That is likely to change, of course. After all, CompuServe has now integrated its Web browser into the CompuServe Information Manager (CIM) software package.

CompuServe's WinCIM and the Internet.

Browsing the Web via CompuServe may not be the same seamless process you'll experience on America Online. But it is much better than CompuServe's original procedure of forcing users to sign on once to use the system's proprietary features, sign off, and then sign on again using the Spry Mosaic software supplied by CompuServe (or some other browser) to access the Web. Now you can do anything you want in a single online session.

The POCIA List of ISPs

Although it is not the only such list, the Providers of Commercial Internet Access or POCIA list is considered one of the best of its kind. It's organized by the area code an ISP serves. Here's an example of the kind of information you will find for each company providing access within a particular area code:

510	Aimnet Information Services	408 257 0900	**info@aimnet.com**
510	BTR Communications Company	415 966 1429	**support@btr.com**
510	Community ConneXion - NEXUS-Berkeley	510 549 1383	**info@c2.org**
510	Direct Net Access Incorporated	510 649 6110	**support@dnai.com**
510	Exodus Communications, Inc.	408 522 8450	**info@exodus.net**

Notice the e-mail addresses that follow the phone numbers here. Generally, you can send a blank or short message to each address and receive in your e-mail mailbox a reply outlining the subscription options and rates charged by the company.

The ISP Option

Once you've explored the Internet via AOL, Prodigy, or CompuServe and have developed a level of confidence, it's time to consider switching to an Internet Service Provider (ISP) of the sort discussed in Chapter 5. Here are the steps to follow:

1. Get a copy of the POCIA list—the Providers of Commercial Internet Access directory list.

See the Internet Toolkit and Glossbrenner's Choice Appendix for instructions on ordering a copy on disk. Or, if you already have an account with one of the Big Three or some other system, you can request the latest copy using e-mail. For complete instructions, send a blank or one-line message to **info@celestin.com**.

2. Select an ISP.

The two most important considerations in selecting an ISP are whether or not you will have to pay long distance telephone charges to connect with it and what you will be charged by the ISP.

Prices may have changed, but at this writing, we can summarize the ideal ISP in a single sentence: Go with a company that lets you place a local call at 28.8 Kbps using any Internet-compatible program you like to connect with a PPP account on the system, and that charges about $20 a month for virtually unlimited access to the Internet at any time of day or night.

PPP, incidentally, stands for "Point-to-Point Protocol," a procedure for making a connection that is newer and faster than the old SLIP or Serial Line Internet Protocol that preceded it.

At this writing, the ISP industry is very much in flux and prices and policies are all over the map. But what we've described here is the emerging standard.

In general, it is likely to be a while before your local television cable company begins to offer Internet access. And, for most people, there is no need to think about "high-speed" ISDN (Integrated Services Digital Network) connections and the expenses they involve. Your ISP is likely to charge you more for such a connection, and you will have to pay your local phone company $20 or more a month for an ISDN line. Not to mention the installation fee and the need to buy an ISDN "modem."

3. Check the newsgroup *alt.internet.access.wanted.*

Use your account on AOL or another consumer system to tap into the newsgroup **alt.internet.access.wanted**. The messages posted to this group may alert you to ISPs that may have been overlooked by the assemblers of the POCIA list.

This newsgroup also gives you the opportunity to post a message saying something like "I'm in Yardley, Pennsylvania—area code 215. Can anyone recommend a good Internet service provider in this area?" Or, "I'm thinking of signing up with Voicenet in Ivyland, PA. Has anyone had any experience with this ISP?"

Ten Questions to Ask an ISP

Here are ten questions you should be sure to ask any Internet Service Provider before agreeing to pay them any money:

1. What costs are involved? Is there a one-time account setup fee? A fee for software?

2. Is there a free trial period? Can I get a full refund if I decide to cancel during this period?

3. What is the monthly charge, and how many hours of connect time do I get with that? What is the charge for each additional hour?

4. Can I connect making a local, non-toll call?

5. Are all your connections at 28.8 Kbps? If not, when will they be?

6. Will my connection be a PPP (Point-to-Point Protocol) or a SLIP (Serial Line Internet Protocol) or something else? (A PPP connection is preferred.)

7. Can I use any kind of TCP/IP-compatible Internet software? Or must I use your proprietary program?

8. How easy is the software to install? Will a real person be available by phone to help me if I run into trouble?

9. Is customer support toll-free? What hours is support available? Is support limited to just certain Internet programs like Netscape and Mosaic? Do you have any online support of the sort found in one of the Internet Forums on CompuServe, AOL, and Prodigy?

10. Is it possible for me to have my own "domain name?" If so, what is the cost of having you handle the registration process? What about my own World Wide Web page? Is there a charge for this? (A domain name is like a vanity license plate. With your own domain name the e-mail address you use on your business cards can be **bill@widgets.com**, assuming you work for Widgets, Inc., instead of **bill@omni.voicenet.com** or **bill578@aol.com**, and so on.)

Conclusion

Basically, if you are new to the Internet or new to the online world in general, start with America Online. Put a kitchen timer next to your computer and set it for one hour at a time. Then sign on to AOL and explore the Internet locations discussed later in this book.

If you hold yourself to no more than 10 hours a month, you'll be in for $25 a month. This is not outrageous, particularly when you consider the customer support (on the phone and online) that is available.

Do this for three months, and then reassess. You will have spent a total of 40 hours (10 free when you sign up and 30 paid hours thereafter) and paid a total of $75. Again, with the guidance and suggestions supplied in other chapters, that's plenty of time for you to decide whether the Net and the Web are for you or not.

If you decide that none of this is for you, cancel your AOL subscription. If you decide that you are a heavy Internet user, then you pretty much have to switch to an ISP, if only to protect your bank account.

Follow the steps presented here and in Chapter 5 for opening an account with an Internet service provider. But hold onto your AOL account for a month or two. Remember, ISPs are not famous for offering great customer service.

So you may find it convenient to keep paying AOL $9.95 a month a little longer to assure yourself of access to that system's online and telephone customer service. After all, at 10:00 PM, the offices of your local ISP are likely to be closed. Any questions will have to wait until tomorrow. But if you are still on AOL, you can sign on and go to one of the 24-hour customer support chat rooms to get your question answered!

two

What *Are* the Main Internet Features?

7

Probably the biggest mistake any new Internet user can make is to assume that the Internet is somehow a much larger version of CompuServe, America Online, or some other commercial system. It's big, alright, but unlike any of the Big Three commercial systems, the Internet was not conceived as a collection of features that could be neatly packaged and offered to the public.

Instead, the Internet just . . . well, it just grew. No executive convened a committee and said, "Okay, folks, we want to design an online service. What features should it have?" Far from it.

An Evolutionary Feature Set

The features you will find on the Internet today are the result of a consensus in the original Internet community. In years past, one person would write a program that would do something and then put it out on the Net. System administrators would test the program and reject it or add it to the list of features offered to their users.

Inevitably, someone else would come along and edit or add to the original programming to improve things. And so the feature would grow and develop.

The Original Computer Nut's Sandbox

With no prejudice implied, it must be understood by all that the original Internet was the biggest damned sandbox any computer nut could imagine playing in. You could do almost *anything*, and the Net community would be the judge of whether it lived or died or was relegated to an electronic backwater somewhere.

The Leading Internet Features

The Internet's recent popularity and visibility, however, have dramatically increased the speed with which new Net features are developed and old standbys are made much easier to use. For example, in July 1994, Random House published our book *Internet Slick Tricks*. Of that book's 271 pages, only three were devoted to the World Wide Web. That's because at the time, the Web was just barely on the scope.

Most of the features you will encounter have evolved from the original Internet community of users, and it is important to know what those features are.

Today, of course, the Web is everywhere. And as Web browser programs like Netscape Navigator add more and more features, the need to load or specify a separate program for each Internet feature you want to use (sending and receiving e-mail, downloading files, "Telnetting" to another location, and so on) is rapidly disappearing.

Whether a World Wide Web browser program can indeed be all things to all people remains to be seen. The old phrase, "jack of all trades, but master of none," comes to mind. But this is definitely the trend.

Tread Softly on the Net

Like any small, relatively close-knit community, the Internet's first users developed informal "rules" and set ways of doing things. Don't type in all capital letters because it is considered SHOUTING. Don't post a message to a newsgroup that has nothing to do with the newsgroup's topic. Make an effort to look for answers on your own before posting a question.

That's why old-time Internauts tend to resent the recent "invasion" of AOL, CompuServe, and Prodigy subscribers. From their perspective, the barbarians are not only at the gate, they're also over the wall and into the sacred sandbox itself! For some, it's as if dozens of busloads of country bumpkins had suddenly driven across the manicured golf greens of their private club, boorishly demanding "What's for dinner?"

For their part, the newbies can't be expected to know that they are violating norms and customs, which is why we're alerting you to that possibility here. To avoid being "flamed"—having someone say nasty things to and about you online—tread softly until you learn the lay of the land.

Still, it is important to remember that most of the features you will encounter have evolved from the original Internet community of users, and it is important to know what those features are:

1. Electronic mail
As you know from Chapter 2, you can use the Net to exchange e-mail messages with people all over the planet, instantly.

2. World Wide Web
The Web turns your computer screen into something that looks like a magazine page, complete with fancy text fonts, photos, and graphics. It is to standard, text-based online communications what Windows is to DOS.

3. Discussion groups
These are officially known as "newsgroups" on the Net. Read and contribute questions, answers, and information on any topic you can imagine. They're sometimes referred to as "Usenet newsgroups" or "Net news." In any event, there are over 15,000 of them!

4. Mailing lists
Internet mailing lists make it easy to automatically distribute a message, an article, or some other text file to everyone who "subscribes" to the list.

Mailing lists are like newsgroups in breadth of topic, but everyone on the list gets every contribution, whether they want it or not.

5. Subject menus

On the Net, this feature is called "Gopher." A Gopher is a menu system that someone has created to make it easier for you to locate and use Internet resources.

There are three things to remember about Gophers. First, each Gopher menu is *unique*. Second, Gopher menus typically embrace all the other features of the Internet. You can use a Gopher to "Telnet" to a location or to "FTP" a file or to do just about anything else—as long as it's on the Gopher menu. Third, you can access any Gopher using your World Wide Web browser software.

6. Free software and other files

In Netspeak, the feature that lets you download a file into your machine is called "FTP" or "File Transfer Protocol" (also called "anonymous FTP"). Once you find text, computer programs, and graphics files, you can transfer them to your location.

7. Remote logon or "Telnet"

This feature lets you log on to a computer connected to the Internet. What you see once you get there depends on the Telnet address you have used. A good example is Telnetting to a location and being able to search a college library's card catalogue.

Conclusion

You now have an excellent overview of the leading Internet features. In Part 3 of this book, we'll show you how to really make good use of each of them.

But before we can do that, we need to introduce you to the main tool you'll want to use to tap most of those features—a Web browser program. We'll start with an introduction to the World Wide Web itself and to the browser software you'll use to access it.

Internet Features Off the Beaten Path

If you're a new user, there's no way to know which of the many Internet features you may hear about are truly important. In reality, the seven features cited in this chapter are the only ones most people will ever need to know about.

But you may encounter references to Finger, IRC, MUDs and MUSEs, and Whois. Here's a quick rundown. If you need to know more, check the Net itself by posting questions in the newsgroups cited here or in the newsgroup **news.newusers.questions**. You might also want to check the clubs, forums, or special interest groups devoted to the Internet on the Big Three systems.

• Finger

This is an old UNIX command that tells a given system to send you a person's full name, phone number, land address, and any other information that user may want others to have. Its original purpose was to allow professors to tell their students the days and times of their office hours and other similar information.

In addition to having the right software, to use Finger you must know the person's name or e-mail address and the host system he or she uses to access the Net. Many systems disable Finger to protect users' privacy, so you're likely to find it of limited value.

• IRC

Internet Relay Chat is rather like global CB radio with an unlimited number of channels and real-time conversations. There are hundreds of IRC "servers" located all over the world, and you can hop among them at will. International scope is the main benefit of IRC. Otherwise, you will find that it is quite crude compared to the chat features offered by the Big Three. Check the newsgroup **alt.irc** for more information.

• MUDs

MUD stands for "Multi-User Dungeon," an Internet feature that uses IRC to offer text-based role-playing games of the *Dungeons and Dragons* variety. Variations include Multi-User Dungeon Object-Oriented (MOO), Multi-User Shared Hallucination (MUSH), Multi-User Shared Environment (MUSE), and more. If this subculture is of interest, check the newsgroup **rec.games.mud** for more information.

• Whois

If you know a person's name or e-mail address, you can log on to a "Whois server" and search its database of directory information. If the person is listed there, you will find his or her land address, phone number, name, and e-mail address. Trouble is, there are hundreds of Whois servers, and there is no guarantee that the person you're looking for is listed on any of them.

Welcome to the World Wide Web!

8

The World Wide Web is without a doubt the hottest—or the "coolest"—of all Internet features. As we said earlier, the Web is to conventional, text-based computer communications what Microsoft Windows is to conventional text-based DOS computing. The World Wide Web, in short, is a "graphical user interface" for the Internet.

The Web is much less complicated than it may at first appear. But we'll save the revelations for later. Let's suppose instead that you're a parent living in Ohio, and your son or daughter is a junior in high school and is thus beginning to look at colleges.

Naturally, you will want to send for brochures, course catalogues, and the like from the schools your child is considering. But today, you and your kid can tap the World Wide Web to get additional information about a college or university, most of which does not appear in standard print materials.

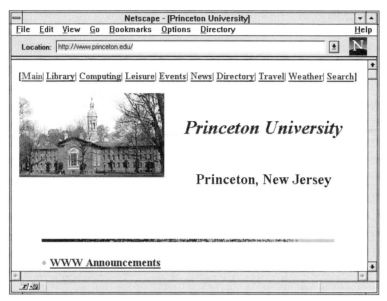

Princeton University: goin' back to Old Nassau!

What's It Look Like?

As an example, look at the figure above of Princeton University's Nassau Hall. This is the World Wide Web "home page" for Princeton University. It appeared on our screen because we connected with the Internet and keyed in **http://www.princeton.edu** to point our browser program to that address.

Within seconds, the screen you see here began to appear. You can do the same thing using the Web browser packages supplied by America Online, Prodigy, and CompuServe.

"Hypertext" Hot Links

The photo is of Nassau Hall, Princeton's "signature building." A pretty picture, but so what? Well, notice that just above this photo is a line that reads "Main," "Library," "Computing," and so on. If you were to move your mouse pointer over any of these words and click, you would be taken to a page containing information about the feature you selected.

That's one way to get information about Princeton. But notice, too, that there's a slider bar on the far right to make it easy for you to scroll up or down through the page you're on right now.

Use the slider, and you will eventually come to the screen entitled "The University." You can click on any of the items on this menu, whether it's the Orange Key Tour or Course Information, and be whisked instantly to a page containing relevant information and images.

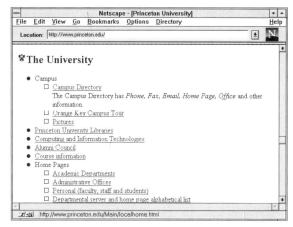

The University and hotlinked information.

Among other topics, you'll find information about the Princeton area, including train schedules, names of hotels and restaurants, weather, and what's playing at local movie theaters. You'll also find a page for the Princeton University Band.

The band is a sentimental favorite of your co-authors because, back in 1970, Alfred was one of its managers and Emily was in the audience at a performance at Wilson College. We met for the first time at a "make-your-own sundaes" mixer held after the show.

"Multimedia" Sound and More

But there's an even better reason for showing you the band's Web home page. On this page, you'll see the word "schedule" underlined. If you click on that, you will be presented with the band's current schedule, of course.

But if you use the slider bar to scroll down the page, you will come to a list of songs, marches, and tunes recorded by the band. As long as you have a SoundBlaster or other multimedia sound player in your Windows/Intel-style, or "Wintel," computer, you can click on "Goin' Back" and the

A long, hard look at the Princeton University Band.

music of this Princeton anthem will begin playing through your computer's speakers. (Macintosh users have sound capability built in and won't need any special equipment.)

Although not part of the Princeton page (at least at this writing), full-motion video clips can be downloaded and played on your computer's screen at other sites on the World Wide Web. And on Princeton's page, as on most other Web pages, you will find many "hot link" buttons you can click on to go to a completely different "Web site."

Give It a Try!

The World Wide Web has gotten a lot of coverage in the press and on television, so there's a good chance that you've already seen people using it. But there's nothing like doing it yourself. So give it a try.

If you're on America Online, sign on, enter Control-K to bring up the Keyword box, and type in the word **web**. AOL's World Wide Web browser should then appear. If it doesn't or if you get an error message, you may have to upgrade your AOL software, so do a Control-K again and specify **upgrade** to be taken to a screen from which you can download the necessary software. (On CompuServe key in **go webcentral**, and on Prodigy jump to **www**.)

When you're all set, point your browser program to any of the locations listed below. Just be sure to key in the address exactly as it is shown here. Unfortunately, World Wide Web addresses are case-sensitive, so if you see capital letters in an address ("YALE"), you must use them:

Arizona State University	**http://info.asu.edu:80/**
Denison University	**http://louie.cc.denison.edu**
Harvard University	**http://www.harvard.edu**
Indiana University	**http://cee.indiana.edu**
Kent State University	**http://vishnu.educ.kent.edu**
MIT	**http://www.mit.edu:8001/people/ cdemello/univ.html**
Princeton University	**http://www.princeton.edu**
Stanford University	**http://www.stanford.edu**

University of Pennsylvania	**http://ccat.sas.upenn.edu**
University of Virginia	**http://gwis.virginia.edu**
Yale University	**http://www.cs.yale.edu/HTML/ YALE/Home.html**

Most colleges and universities have Web home pages. So if there is some particular institution you want to check, you might try an address in the format **http://www.whatsamattau.edu** where "whatsamat-tau" is the name of the target college or university. Don't worry if your guessed address does not work. We'll show you how to search for the right address later in this book.

The key thing right now is to sign on to a Web site and just play! Move your mouse pointer to any item of interest, click on it, and see what happens. If you want to backtrack, just move your mouse pointer up to "Go" (or "Navigate") on the command line at the top of the screen and click. That will produce a drop-down menu of the names of the pages you have previously visited, and you can click on one of them.

Ten minutes of actually *using* the World Wide Web can be worth ten hours of reading about it. So take the time to actually try the Web and get a feel for it.

All About Web "Browser" Programs

9

There is little doubt that the graphical user interface that has been added to the Internet by the World Wide Web and Web browser programs played a major role in the Internet frenzy that has gripped so many people in recent years. But browser software is still evolving rapidly.

Yet, while all browsers are definitely not created equal, whether it's Netscape or Mosaic or the browsers offered by AOL, Prodigy, Compu-Serve, the Microsoft Network, and the rest, they all operate in essentially the same way.

No magic is involved. A Web site doesn't send you anything that computers haven't been sending over the phone for decades. Fundamentally, in fact, a World Wide Web page physically consists of nothing more than a plain old text file.

Stripping Off the Mask

When you point your browser software to the address **http://www.princeton.edu**, the one we used in the last chapter, what is actually sent to your computer is this:

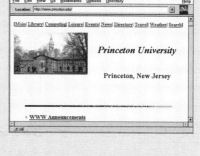

```
<HTML>
<HEAD>
<TITLE>Princeton University</TITLE></HEAD>
<BODY>
<A NAME="top"></A>
<CENTER><H4>
[<A HREF="http://www.princeton.edu/">Main</A>|
<A HREF="http://infoshare1.princeton.edu:2003">Library</A>|
<A HREF="http://www.princeton.edu/Main/computing.html">Computing</A>|
<A HREF="http://www.princeton.edu/Main/entertainment.html">Leisure</A>|
<A HREF="http://www.princeton.edu/Main/events.html">Events</A>|
<A HREF="http://www.princeton.edu/Main/news.html">News</A>|
    .
    .
    .
```

Okay, so this might look scary and complex with all those angle brackets and "http" and "www" thingies all over the place. But if you take a moment to actually *read* what you see here, it begins to make an odd kind of sense. For example, "<TITLE>Princeton University</TITLE></HEAD>" may not be intuitively clear, but you can kind of see what they're getting at.

The big question is: How does this plain text get transformed into different type styles, type fonts, and graphical images of the sort we've seen in this book so far?

The answer, of course, is that a special piece of software—the Web browser programs you've heard about—are designed to accept these textual instructions as their marching orders. In our case, it was the browser program called Netscape Navigator that accepted the text shown in the sidebar "Stripping Off the Mask" and transformed it into the screens you saw in the last chapter.

When you log on to a Web site with your browser program, the site sends you a text file that determines how and where headlines and body text will appear. It also sends you the graphic image files (photos, drawings, digital scans, etc.) that will be displayed. You won't normally see anything as raw as the text we've shown you here.

The Lowest Common Denominator

Think about this for just a minute. If many different makes and models of computers—Macintoshes, IBM mainframes, old Kaypros and Commodores, DEC VAXes, and DOS/Windows machines—are to be able to exchange information, everyone's got to agree on a standard. In the online world, that would be the American Standard Code for Information Interchange, or ASCII (pronounced "as-key").

Computers communicate with numbers. So the ASCII code is really nothing more than a chart that assigns a number to every letter of the alphabet. And everyone agrees on the contents of the chart. Thus, if any computer anywhere receives the number "68," it knows to display a capital letter "D." If it receives the number "100," it knows to display a lowercase "d." And so on.

Your browser program and your particular collection of fonts determine how a given page will actually appear.

But what determines what that capital "D" will actually *look* like on your screen? What typeface will be used? How large will the letter be? Will it be in bold or italic?

The software you are using at the time controls these variables. And, of course, you control the software when you tell it which fonts you want it to use for which text. Most communications software programs can use any of the TrueType or other fonts you've got loaded into your computer.

Enter the Web

Web browser programs work in much the same way. But there's a crucial difference.

Like magazine pages, Web pages are *designed*. For example, at this writing, three different sizes of headings are available, numbered one through three. So the person designing the Web page might write "<H1>Welcome to My Page!</H1>" to specify the largest heading at the top of the page and might use "<H2>" and "<H3>" farther down the page.

These instructions are part of "HyperText Markup Language" or "HTML." An HTML text file is what gets sent to you when you log on to any Web site. But it is your browser program and your particular collection of fonts that determine how a given page will actually appear.

Still, a heading the designer has specified as an "<H1>" should be bigger on your screen than one tagged as "<H3>," even though the exact typeface used on your system and on our system may be different.

All browser programs have the ability to display the graphic images that a Web site sends. But some also come equipped to play sound and even video clips. Others are designed to use third-party "helper" programs, supplied by you, to accomplish these feats. Fortunately, with Netscape setting the pace, browser software is rapidly evolving toward a standard set of features.

Hypertext and the Web

All browser programs have a "hypertext" or "hot link" capability, however. This simply means that when you see a word or phrase that is highlighted by being in a different color than the text that surrounds it, you can click on that spot and be taken instantly to some other "page" or to an entirely different Web location.

For example, imagine a page devoted to fruit. The word "apples" is highlighted, so you click on it and are taken to a new page devoted to apples. There you find lots of information about apples in general, but the phrase "Granny Smith" is highlighted and therefore "clickable," so you click, and you're taken to a new page containing a lot of information about Australia, where that particular variety of apple originated.

The Australian page might also mention "New Zealand," so you click on that and are taken to a page describing that lovely country. That page contains "lamb" as one of its hypertext hot links, so you click on that and are taken to yet another new page devoted to the care and feeding of lambs and sheep. And—what's this?—"border collie." You click on that and are taken to a page devoted to this most intelligent of dogs.

You're a long way from "fruit," but what an experience! When you understand that each of the various pages suggested here can be physically located on a computer anywhere on the globe, and that you can connect with any of them instantly, you begin to see why they call it the "World Wide Web." You can also see why they call the programs that make this kind of electronic journey possible "browsers." In the next chapter, we'll show you how to make the most of your browser.

Making the Most of Your Browser

10

We know that hypertext links were the essence of the original design for the World Wide Web and that graphics and fonts were not. But even today, most people are not aware that the second major goal of the Web was to provide a much more uniform interface for using almost all of the leading Internet features.

This needs to be emphasized. In addition to using your favorite World Wide Web browser to access Web pages, you can *also* use it to download files via FTP, access any Gopher menu system, Telnet to any location, read and post messages to newsgroups, and even send (and possibly receive) electronic mail.

The process is quite simple. Just mouse up to the box at the top of the browser screen labeled "Location:" (or go to its equivalent on your browser), click to get the text cursor to appear, and type in a "Uniform Resource Locator" or "URL."

Uniform Resource Locators (URLs) and Such

The URL you enter tells your browser program what feature you want to use (FTP, Telnet, etc.) and where you want to go to use it. Naturally, naming something like this the target "address" or the "feature selector" would be too simple and obvious to suit the typical software designer.

So "URL" it is. Officially, at least. Fact is, most normal people use the terms "address" and "URL" interchangeably, as in "Please give me the address of your Web site."

Here are six of the URLs you should be able to use with your browser. We qualify that statement because, while Netscape can use them all, other browser programs may not yet have caught up. Most will certainly have done so by the time you read this, however. Notice that the newsgroup and mail addresses do not include a pair of forward slashes:

World Wide Web home page	**http://**
Gopher menu system	**gopher://**
Telnet remote access	**telnet://**
File transfers	**ftp://**
Newsgroups	**news:**
Electronic mail	**mailto:**

One final caveat: URLs are *case-sensitive*! We pointed that out in Chapter 8, but it bears repeating, since if you don't pay attention to the upper- and lowercase letters in the URLs you key in, you'll get an error message about the site not existing or some such note. But you won't have a clue that the problem is case-sensitivity.

All of which is to say that you should take special care when entering a URL the first time. Fortunately, as we'll see in a moment, once you've done so successfully, you may never need to do so again. That's because most Web browsers can be told to save the URLs of places you like, making it easy to just point and click the next time you want to visit a spot.

For Intermediate and Advanced Computer Users

In the chapters that follow, we are going to present a lot more information about how to use and make the most of the major Internet features. And, with the exception of e-mail, we will be accessing these features through a Web browser.

If you are a brand-new computer user and a brand-new online user, then we're afraid we must insist that you stop here and turn to the "Web Browser Cookbook" section of this book for the simple, hands-on instructions you need regarding how to use this kind of software.

If you're an intermediate to advanced computer user, however, you may be able to wing it and refer to the "Cookbook" only when you have a question. To help you determine whether you need to consult the "Cookbook" right now or not, we've prepared an informative, entertaining test that will alert you to the main tasks you need to be able to perform using a browser.

The Peachpit Press Home Page Test

Ready? Okay. Sign on to America Online, key in Control-K, and specify **web** when the Keyword box comes up. Or sign on to Prodigy, to CompuServe using CompuServe's Spry Mosaic or other browser, or to your Internet Service Provider (ISP) using Netscape, NetCruiser, or some other browser. However you do it, the goal is to get your Web browser up and running and connected to the Net.

Welcome to the Peachpit Press home page!

Next, point your browser at the following address: **http://www.peachpit.com**. The Peachpit Press home page will appear on your screen. (If you do not know how to do this, opt out of the test now and consult the "Web Browser Cookbook" section at the back of this book.)

Mouse around on this page and click on any item of interest. Whatever you click on will take you to a new page. And once there, you may click on something else that will take you to yet another page. Work at worming your way deep into the nest of pages. Then click on the button labeled "Back" or "Go" at the top of the screen and see if you can figure out how to click your way back to the original Peachpit Press home page.

For extra credit, you might consider clicking on buttons at the top of the screen labeled with terms like "Bookmarks" or "Hotlist" or "Favorite Places" and *adding* the Peachpit Press page to your list. This will save you the trouble of keying in the entire URL address each time you want to return to the given location. You can do this for each

URL you plan to visit frequently.

So in the future, you can click on a button like "Favorite Places" or "Bookmarks," look at the list of locations that will appear on the drop-down menu, and double-click on the one you want to go to.

Saving the Page

Finally, practice "saving the page." Imagine that you have clicked your way through the Peachpit Press Web site and have come upon the page for *The Little Online*

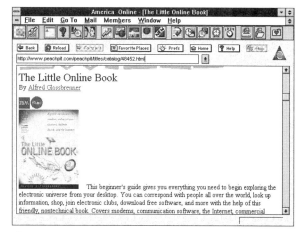

Glossbrenner's Little Online Book *from Peachpit Press.*

Book. Imagine that you would like to save this page on disk. The key is to click on the File menu at the top of your browser's screen and then select "Save" or "Save as" and follow the resulting prompts.

The disk file you save will contain the text, but no graphic images. The text may be in HTML format (littered with angle brackets and codes) or it may be a plain text file. It all depends on your browser's abilities. For example, if you specify .TXT as part of your file name, your browser may save the page as a plain text file. If you don't, you'll probably get HTML.

If you can't get plain text, you may be able to use a program like the DOS utility DE-HTML.EXE to automatically strip all the HTML coding from a file. But we can save that for later. The final thing to note is that if you want to save a graphic image, you may be able to place the mouse pointer on top of it and click on the *right* mouse button. If this causes your browser to give you a drop-down menu to use in saving the file, you're in business! If not, you may need a different browser.

Conclusion

If you can perform the tasks presented here with confidence the second or third time through, then you can consider yourself a Web user of basic proficiency. There is much more to learn in the fine-tuning department, but there is no need to concern yourself with it now. So plunge into the chapters in Part 3.

Sending and Receiving Messages (E-Mail)

11

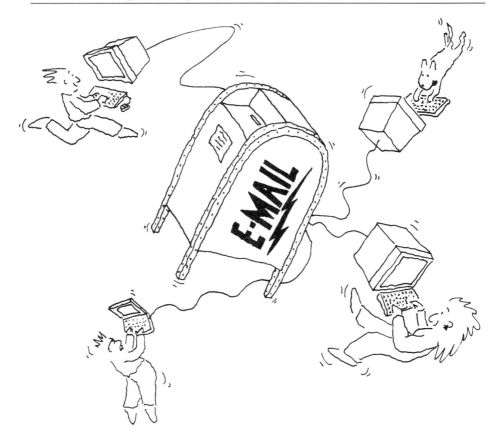

Electronic mail, or e-mail, is without a doubt the most popular of all online and Internet features. And with good reason. First, you can contact anyone who owns a personal computer and has an account on nearly any kind of online system **anywhere in the world!**

Second, you can do so at almost any time of day or night. No need to worry about time zones or whether your recipient will be awake when you are. Just send the message, and they'll pick it up at their convenience.

Third, your message can include not only plain text but also sound clips, graphic images, and even short videotape cuts.

Just imagine: Mommy's in Japan on business when Baby takes her first steps, but Daddy captures it all on videotape. Within moments, the video clip has been digitized, turned into a file, and sent to Mommy via the Internet. She'll be able to view it on her laptop computer the first thing in the morning.

This isn't science fiction. The audio- and video-capture equipment you'll need isn't cheap, but it is widely available. As are the computers and modems needed to bring it all off. Still, the entire process is far from seamless. Some technical savvy is required.

But that won't always be the case. The point is that what we've outlined here can indeed be done by some people today. Tomorrow, it will be a common function for everybody.

Easy E-Mail

Multimedia e-mail is still at the far end of the e-mail spectrum. Most of us merely want to be able to exchange letters and files with friends, relatives, and business associates.

Working with mail on the Big Three systems is really quite simple. It's mostly a matter of clicking on "Mail," keying in an address, typing in your message, and then clicking on "Send." You'll find that things are even easier if you bear a few basic concepts in mind.

How to Figure the Cost of Sending a Message

E-mail isn't *always* the best alternative. If you've got scores of megabytes to send, you'll probably be better off recording the data on floppy disks and sending them via Federal Express or a similar service.

But if you want to send a report consisting of 30 double-spaced typewritten pages across the country, Federal Express will charge you at least $12. First Class postage will run you around $2. But you can send it via the Internet for about three cents, and it will be there instantly!

The trick to estimating the time needed to send a file is to divide the number of bytes in the file by one-tenth of the modem speed. If the file is 56,000 bytes long, for example, and you're communicating at 14,400 bits per second, divide 56,000 by 1,440. You'll find that the answer is about 38 seconds, or about 63 percent of a minute. Since the Big Three charge about five cents a minute, the cost is 63 percent of five cents, or about three cents.

This assumes ideal conditions with no delays, of course. And it doesn't include the time spent signing on to the system and moving to the mail feature. But the actual cost could turn out to be many times this figure, and it would still be a heck of a bargain!

Internet E-Mail Addresses

As part of your account on each of the Big Three systems, you will be given an e-mail address. This is often the same as your account number or name and takes the form "John157" or "Martha-Z." CompuServe uses numbers like "70012,3456," but it has been experimenting with allowing subscribers to select more user-friendly "aliases" like "Billy-Bob" for their e-mail.

Let's assume that you're John157 on America Online. To transform your AOL user name into an Internet e-mail address, all you've got to do is add an "at" sign (@) and "aol.com": **John157@aol.com**. If you're John157 on Prodigy, your Internet e-mail address is: **John157@prodigy.com**.

In Netspeak, everything to the right of the "at" sign is a person's "domain name." It's as if John worked in mythical "AOL Building" in New York City and as if that building had its own internal mail delivery system. Messages from the Internet are dropped off at the first-floor lobby, and then the building's internal system takes over and sees that each message is delivered to the right mailbox.

Three Small Caveats

If you want your *own* domain name, like **john@widgets.com**, you will need to have an account with an ISP (Internet Service Provider) instead of one of the Big Three. You should also know that if you are sending mail to a CompuServe account via the Net, you must replace the comma it contains with a *period*. Thus, if a person's CompuServe account number is **71234,5678**, the Internet address to use would be **71234.5678@compuserve.com**.

Finally, if you need someone's e-mail address, the fastest, easiest way to get it is to call the person on the phone or send a paper letter. In our experience, the so-called "White Pages" Internet directories, like the purely voluntary directories on the Big Three, have a long way to go.

ASCII Text and Binary Files

One of the things that can easily trip up a new user when it comes to electronic mail is being unaware of the difference between *text* files and *binary* files. This sounds kind of scary, but it's not.

The problem is that computers are limited in the number of signals they can generate. So ways have been found to use the same signal for vastly different things. It is, you might say, a question of context.

Playing the Piano

Think of a piano keyboard. There are 88 keys, each of which generates a distinct sound signal when you hit it. That is all the piano has to work with. Most of the time, the piano uses these 88 signals to produce "music." Music can convey all kinds of emotions and other "information," but no one would confuse music with words.

Now suppose someone comes along and says, "You know, I think I can use these 88 sound signals to transmit words. All I've got to do is assign one letter of the alphabet to each signal and make sure that the person listening to these signals is aware of the letter or punctuation mark each signal represents."

The results might sound awful. But then, they were never meant to be heard as music. They were meant to transmit text. The point is: The same set of signals—the 88 notes of a piano—can be used to convey music or they can be used to convey text. The signals are identical in both cases. It is the *context* that is different.

The same is true with text files and binary files.

The identical collection of signals—or bytes—is used for both. But the context is different. A so-called "7-bit" text file, for example, is designed to be viewed by any computer, regardless of make or model, and regardless of the word processing program used. It is as "plain vanilla" as you can get.

A binary file, in contrast, was never *meant* to be viewed by everyone. It may have been prepared as a "document" file by MS Word, WordPerfect, and the like, and be viewable only if you happen to own one of those programs. Or it may be a graphics file that has been saved in a particular graphics format (.GIF, .PCX, .TIF, etc.). It may even be a program file that was created to be run on your computer.

Dealing with Binary Files

There are four things to remember about binary files. First, if you are sending them to someone on the *same* system, they must be uploaded or downloaded using an error-checking protocol. The Prodigy and AOL

Protecting E-Mail Privacy

Electronic mail is not and never has been private. Though it's highly unlikely, you must assume that because someone *can* read your mail, someone *will*. Therefore, whenever you are sending a confidential or sensitive message, you should take the time to encrypt it.

This is easy to do, and the programs needed to do it are widely available via the Big Three or on the Net. In the Glossbrenner's Choice collection, for example, we've put together a disk with everything a DOS or Windows user needs to keep the National Security Agency guessing, including Philip Zimmermann's Pretty Good Privacy (PGP) program.

PGP is also available for Macintosh users. Contact the mail-order firm Educorp at 800-843-9497, or point your Web browser to one of the InfoMac sites at **http://www.tonet.com/~baron/infomac**. InfoMac sites let you search any number of Macintosh file collections. We picked **sumex-aim.stanford.edu** from the list and searched on "pgp." This located a program called mac-pgp-control-10b1-as.hqx, among others. Downloading it was as easy as clicking on the Download button offered by InfoMac.

Encrypting a file is easy. Basically, you create your message and then run an encryption program. The program will ask you to supply a "key" that it can use to control just how it scrambles the file. The key might be "whale" or "xyzzy" or anything else. As long as your recipient has the same program, and as long as you give the person the key (either by voice phone or by a separate e-mail message), he or she will be able to transform the gibberish back into readable text in an instant.

programs handle this automatically, as do programs like the Compu-Serve Information Manager (CIM) and its imitators.

Second, if you're using a Big Three account to send binary files to an Internet address, you will probably have to first convert them to plain 7-bit ASCII text. That's because not all systems that are connected to the Net can handle binary files. But every system can handle plain ASCII text.

The conversion to and from binary to text format may be performed automatically by your e-mail program when you tell it to send a file or when you receive a file. Or you may have to do it manually with a "UU-CODE" program. (See the Internet Toolkit and Glossbrenner's Choice Appendix for information on the UU-CODE process.)

Third, do not assume that your correspondent uses the same word processing software you do! If the person does indeed use the same program, then you can save a file as a formatted document, convert it to 7-bit ASCII text, and send it via the Net. Otherwise, be sure that you save the file as a plain ASCII text file. If you don't, your correspondent probably won't be able to read it.

Finally, there's the matter of message size. Some systems hooked into the Internet can handle anything of any length that you throw at them via electronic mail. But many cannot. That's why you should limit the size of any given message to no more than 64,000 characters or bytes (64K). That's the equivalent of about 35 pages of double-spaced text, assuming 65 characters per line and 28 text lines per page.

Since the UU-CODE text version of many binary files frequently exceeds 64K, UU-CODE programs typically divide things up into multiple 64K messages. As long as you make sure that you send all of them, your recipient's UU-CODE program will have no trouble automatically reassembling them in the proper order as it converts them back to binary files.

Conclusion

Electronic mail is such an important online feature that we have spent a bit more time with it than usual. You now have the major tools needed to begin using e-mail right away. If you need an address to use for your initial test message, send a short message to **books@mailback.com**. If all goes well, within a minute or two you'll have a new letter in your mailbox. (We'll leave you to discover its contents on your own.)

SO, BEN, WHICH WAY DO YOU LEAN ON A LOGO?

A   B

UNITED STATES POSTAL SERVICE

Discussion Groups on Every Topic (Newsgroups)

12

MEETING ON THE WEB LIKE WE DID, I WAS, OF COURSE, SLIGHTLY SKEPTICAL.

SILLY YOU.

According to a survey conducted late in 1995 by International Data Corporation (IDC), some 87 percent of Internet users at companies use e-mail, 63 percent use the World Wide Web, and only 40 percent use newsgroups. Still, we would wager that newsgroups are the most loved Internet feature. Indeed, some users are so passionate about their favorite newsgroups that they have established a newsgroup "culture" complete with its own "Netiquette," or code of behavior.

Others rely on newsgroups to get the FAQs (files of Frequently Asked Questions, pronounced "facts") on almost any aspect of the Net. Still others find newsgroups highly addictive. Years ago, in fact, one of our clients at Bell Labs told us she'd had to fire her assistant because she spent the entire day reading the "Net news."

Back to the Beginning

Internet newsgroups—or Net news as they are sometimes called—are transmitted among sites by a program called "Usenet," which is a contraction of the words "USENIX" (the name of the large UNIX user group) and "network." The program was designed by Ellis, Truscott, and Bellovin in 1979 at the University of North Carolina. Its original purpose was to automatically transmit news about various aspects of the UNIX world, hence the name "newsgroups."

The articles that people post circulate like dust particles in the jet stream. The flow of messages among Internet sites is constant, and that stream encompasses the entire world.

Things have grown far beyond news about UNIX today. The last time we checked, there were over 15,000 newsgroups, only about 30 of which are devoted to discussion of the UNIX operating system.

Today, there are newsgroups devoted to every imaginable subject—everything from the TV shows *Beavis and Butt-Head* and *The Rockford Files* to tips on brewing your own beer or improving your sex life.

Newsgroup Basics

One can easily get lost in newsgroup esoterica. So we'll stick to the main road. Here, we will lay out the most essential points, and then, in Chapter 19, we'll show you how to find any group of interest to you. The essential points include:

1. Conceptually, newsgroups are merely "player piano rolls" of messages, or "articles" in Netspeak.

Each group is devoted to a particular topic. The comments Internet users may want to make about that topic are posted one after the other in a long roll. They are thus far less sophisticated than the SIGs, forums, clubs, and the like you'll find on the Big Three.

2. No one controls the newsgroups on the Net.

The articles that people post circulate like dust particles in the jet stream. The flow of messages among Internet sites is constant, and that stream encompasses the entire world. Some groups are "moderated,"

Newsgroup Names and Hierarchies

Newsgroups are divided into topics. Each main topic is further divided, and the result is often divided again and again, as areas are created for discussions of ever-greater specificity.

For example, a group called **alt.music** might be formed to discuss music in general. But as people really get into the swing of things, some may decide that they really want to focus on baroque, jazz, or hip-hop. So **alt.music.baroque** might be formed, along with **alt.music.jazz** and **alt.music.hip-hop**. And so on.

The period is pronounced "dot." So you would say, "alt-dot-music-dot-jazz" when referring to the group **alt.music.jazz**.

Here are what are likely to be the topic categories of greatest interest to most people:

alt.	Alternative newsgroups—basically, topics that don't fit neatly anywhere else. Many Usenet sites don't carry these groups. This is where to look for everything from the sexy stuff to the truly offbeat.
biz.	The accepted place for advertisements, marketing, and other commercial postings. Product announcements, product reviews, demo software, and so forth can be found here.
clari.	ClariNet is a commercial service. For a subscription fee paid by the site that carries its feed, ClariNet provides the Associated Press and Reuters newswires, newspaper columns, and lots of other goodies.
comp.	Topics of interest to both computer professionals and hobbyists, including computer science, software source code, and information on hardware and software systems.
misc.	Groups addressing themes not easily classified under any of the other headings, or groups that incorporate themes from multiple categories.
news.	Groups concerned with the Usenet network and software (not current affairs, as you might think).
rec.	Groups oriented toward the arts, hobbies, and recreational activities. A great place to look for miles and miles of jokes.

however, which means that all postings must be approved by an individual or a committee before they appear to the group as a whole.

3. Not all systems that are connected to the Internet carry all groups.
For example, we have not checked, but it is possible that you might be able to read some newsgroups on AOL that are not available via Compu-Serve—and vice versa. It's all a question of which groups the people who

run a given system have decided to make available. Certainly, the topics focused on by some groups could be considered in bad taste. But it is much more likely that the number of groups made available to you via a given system will be limited by the time all that text takes to transmit and the huge amount of disk space it occupies once it arrives!

4. Anyone can post a new article or a reply to an article on almost any group.

Taken together, a new article and the replies it generates form a "message thread." The only limitations are that the postings be appropriate to the group, that no single posting be longer than the equivalent of about 15 single-spaced pages of text, and that you use plain, 7-bit ASCII text. (Prepare your message with your favorite word processor, but be sure to save it in "non-document" mode.)

5. Proper "Netiquette" dictates that you read a newsgroup for a week or more to get a sense of what it is all about before you post your first article or message.

After all, the answer to your question may already exist in someone else's "post." Use upper- and lowercase letters. Using full caps is considered SHOUTING! Do not try to advertise a product or service in a group unless you are certain you won't get "flamed" for doing so. (Flaming in this sense means that group members will post nasty messages about you to the group and send you nasty e-mail.)

Conclusion

You can use one of the Big Three systems to read newsgroups. America Online in particular has a very easy-to-use newsgroup feature. Or you can use your favorite browser by specifying the URL **news:** followed by the name of the group. (Note that the **news:** URL does not use any slashes.)

Many browsers, like Netscape Navigator 2.x, include powerful newsreading modules that prepare a hierarchically arranged "clickable" list of article topics and subsidiary responses, and responses to responses. For more information and an example of what this looks like, please see the "Web Browser Cookbook" at the back of this book.

More Discussion, More Topics—by E-Mail! (Mailing Lists)

13

Electronic mail is one means of exchanging ideas. Newsgroups are another. In this chapter, we'll consider a third, the Internet feature called "mailing lists."

All About Mailing Lists

Internet mailing lists work just like a conventional paper-mail mailing list: Once your name has been added to a list, messages sent to the list will begin to appear in your electronic mailbox automatically.

Regardless of your interests, you may find that joining a mailing list is like becoming a member of a perpetual symposium. The discussions are ongoing, and every member gets a copy of what every other member has contributed.

In general, the main difference between mailing lists and newsgroups is that mailing list subscribers get a copy of everything, whether they want it or not. As part of a newsgroup, in contrast, you are free to pick and choose what you want to read.

Still, when you want to read a newsgroup, you've got to make an effort to go to a newsgroup and select articles of interest. With a mailing list, once you have subscribed, no additional effort is required. Articles turn up in your mailbox automatically.

Where Did They Come From?

Mailing lists exist because the software that ran one of the major networks that became part of the Internet could not handle newsgroups. That network was and is called "Bitnet," and it is the network that links most colleges and universities.

Bitnet users invented the mailing list and the "list server." A list server is a computer that looks for special words in the subject line or the body text of the letters it receives. Upon finding them, it automatically adds the name of the letter's sender to a given mailing list.

Internet users decided that this was a good idea. So they created automatic list servers of their own. Then some of them created Internet newsgroups to "mirror" Bitnet mailing lists.

Mailing lists are great, but they are all-or-nothing propositions. No mailing list subscriber has any control over what ends up in his or her mailbox. If you subscribe to a list, you get everything.

This second step should not be underestimated. Mailing lists are great, but they are all-or-nothing propositions. No mailing list subscriber has any control over what ends up in his or her mailbox. If you subscribe to a list, you get everything.

When mailing list articles are put into a newsgroup format, however, you can look at the article titles, decide which ones you want to read, and ignore the rest.

Getting a List of Mailing Lists

The first step in taking advantage of mailing lists is to get a list that includes the names of lists that exist, their subject areas, and their subscription information. Two of the most comprehensive and well-respected files are the SRI List of Lists and Stephanie da Silva's Publicly Accessible Mailing Lists (PAML) list.

You can get the PAML list by pointing your Web browser at **http://www.neosoft.com/internet/paml**. Or you can enter **ftp://rtfm.mit.edu** and follow the path **/pub/usenet/news.answers/mail/mailing-lists/**. Or you can find it in the newsgroups **news.lists** and **news.answers**.

You can get the SRI list by pointing your browser at **ftp://sri.com** and following the path **/netinfo/interest-groups**. You can get it by e-mail by sending a message to **mail-server@sri.com** and including the line

Mind Your Addresses!

Mailing lists have two—count 'em, two—addresses. If you want to have your name added to the subscription list, you send an e-mail message requesting that to the list's *subscription* address. But when you want to make a contribution of your own, you send it as an e-mail message to the *list* address.

The fine points are spelled out in the introductory paragraphs offered by the SRI list and the PAML list. For example, you may be told that to add your name to a given list, you must send an e-mail message to the subscription address containing the phrase "subscribe listname," where "listname" is the name of the target list.

These two types of addresses are clearly spelled out in most write-ups of available mailing lists. But if you're new to the Net, you might miss the distinction between them.

"send interest-groups" in the body of the message. And you can look for it in the newsgroups **news.lists** and **news.answers**.

The overlap between these lists is surprisingly small. So you really need copies of both of them. As a convenience, they are available from Glossbrenner's Choice on a set of disks called "Mailing List Essentials." See the Internet Toolkit and Glossbrenner's Choice Appendix for details.

Conclusion: The Sound of Distant Thunder

At this point, no one would blame you for feeling that maybe you've stumbled into "Jurassic Park," and that the ground-shaking thuds you hear and feel in the distance—the ones that set pools of water to vibrating—signal the approach of a genuine information monster.

We've done e-mail. The World Wide Web. Newsgroups. Mailing lists. And that's just the Internet. We haven't talked about the topic-specific Special Interest Groups, file libraries, chat rooms, and other features offered by the Big Three. You have every right to feel that the Tyrannosaurus rex of electronic information is approaching—and that it is about to eat you alive.

Fortunately, tools—make that "weapons"—exist that can give you a fighting chance of finding and using the information you want and need. The Information Monster *can* be tamed. And the best place to start is with a humble little "Gopher," as we will see in the next chapter.

Sample Mailing List Descriptions

Because most mailing lists originated on the collegiate Bitnet network, they tend to be rather scholarly in general. But it's not all Proust and Poussin, as the following descriptions from the SRI list will show. Notice that each listing includes a "subscription address." That's the address to which you send your e-mail request containing "subscribe listname" in the body, where "listname" is the name of the target list.

```
HANDYMAN-HINTS
  Subscription Address: MAJORDOMO@CEDAR.CIC.NET
  Owner: Ara Rubyan <arar@dial.cic.net>
  Description:
    HANDYMAN-HINTS is a moderated mailing list on subjects related to Handy-
    man Hints for do-it-yourselfers. One of the contributing editors is Glenn
    Haege, widely hailed as America's Master Handyman. Glenn's radio show,
    "Ask the Handyman," has been on WXYT-AM in the Detroit market since 1983.

LATE-SHOW-NEWS
  Subscription Address: LISTSERV@AMERICAN.EDU
  Owner: Aaron Barnhart <barnhart@mcs.com>
  Description:
    LATE-SHOW-NEWS is a moderated mailing list for the distribution of LATE
    SHOW NEWS, a weekly electronic newsletter with facts and opinions on the
    late-night television talk show industry generally, and in particular the
    Late Show with David Letterman. It is published every Tuesday evening to
    several Usenet newsgroups, including alt.fan.letterman and rec.arts.tv.

TRAVEL-L
  Subscription Address: LISTSERV@TREARNPC.EGE.EDU.TR
  Owner: James A. Schaefer <JSchaefer@Grog.RIC.Edu>
  Description:
    TRAVEL-L is a list for the discussion of travel experiences where every-
    one is welcome to recount their adventures or inquire about future trav-
    els. Members of this list come from all over the world, and have very
    different educational, political, religious, and travel experiences.
    Please be sensitive to the wide differences between peoples and their
    customs by carefully wording your inquiries and responses, but use this
    list to share and learn more about these rich differences. The list is
    supported by Ege University in Izmir, Turkey and is NOT a forum to facil-
    itate commercial travel arrangements, and for-profit advertising is not
    welcomed.

WORDPLAY-L
  Subscription Address: MAILSERV@LEVELS.UNISA.EDU.AU
  Owner: Ahsan Hariz <a.hariz@unisa.edu.au>
  Description:
    WordPlay-L is a digest-format list that deals with the usage of words and
    phrases in the English language, including vocabulary, grammar, spelling,
    and pronunciation. Participants will have a chance to debate wording or
    phrasing of a controversial nature and explore the origins of English
    idioms. The list is open to all literary enthusiasts from the purist to
    the slang user. It promises to be intellectually challenging and also
    quite fun, as word games and quizzes can be sent by anyone for all to
    play. It is distributed 3 to 5 times a week.
```

Menus to Help You Find Things (Gopher)

14

Here's a radical statement for you: Gopher, the menu system we first discussed in Chapter 7, may very well be the single best feature on the Internet!

World Wide Web fanatics may draw back in shock and horror, but we can prove our case. And by the time you finish this chapter, we think you'll agree.

Gopher and the Central Problem

Your co-authors have been analyzing and writing about online, electronic information for over 15 years. We know that an incredible amount of information is available electronically. But we also know that much of it is poorly organized—if it's even organized at all—and that can make it extremely difficult to find what you need.

That's why we're so enthusiastic about the Internet's Gopher feature, for a Gopher is a "menu system" prepared by one or more people in an attempt to impose some order on the Internet. There are just a few key points to bear in mind.

Key Gopher Points

First, the Gopher software was written at the University of Minnesota and was made freely available across the Net. People will try to get you to believe that its name is derived from the "Golden Gophers," the name of that university's sports mascot. But don't you believe it. Internet Gophers actually do "go for" some Internet resource when you make a menu selection.

Second, this software arrives as an empty shell. It is like a file cabinet with drawers filled with Pendaflex folders and three-cut manila folders—but nothing is labeled and there is no data or other information. It is up to the administrators and staff at a given Internet site to place labels on the folders and to decide which topics will be covered and how things will be arranged.

Each Gopher is Unique!

The third point follows naturally: Every Gopher menu on the Internet is a unique creation.

Pause for a moment to let that sink in. Imagine that you have a special interest, say, collecting thimbles of all kinds. You want to make it easy for others who share your interest to get information about this hobby.

So you create a menu system. The initial menu might include selections labeled "Books about Thimbles," "Videotapes about Thimbles," and "Welcome to the Thimble Gopher." Someone who clicked on the "Books" menu item would be taken to a submenu containing one item for each of the leading books about this hobby. If they clicked on one of these items, they would be taken to a review of the book. And so on.

Notice, though, that there is no promise of comprehensiveness. You have not claimed to cover every existing book, article, or videotape about the hobby of thimble collecting. You have offered what you personally feel is the best information, or at least the information that you yourself happen to know about.

This same notion applies to every Gopher you will encounter on the Net. We would only add a fourth point. And that is the fact that a Gopher menu can give you access to nearly any feature on the Net, whether it is FTPing a file, Telnetting to some location, reading newsgroups, or something else.

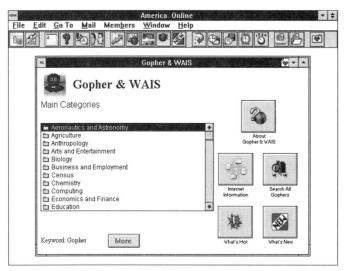

The main Gopher menu on AOL.

A Gopher Example, via AOL

Technically speaking, you access a Gopher by Telnetting to a site. As you may remember, all Telnet does is connect you to a given address. What happens next is up to the program that is set to run when you arrive there. So when you Telnet to a Gopher site, guess which program starts to run? Gopher, of course!

We'll show you how to do this manually, using your favorite browser, in a moment. But let's start with the easiest Gopher of all, the one on America Online.

You can use the keyword "Gopher" on AOL to get to the main gopher screen. Look at all those topics! We scrolled down and chose "Literature and Publications," and a screen of gophers for literature and publications appeared. It is worth taking the time to actually read the names of the Gophers listed here.

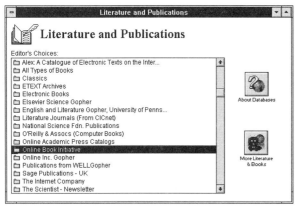

Gophers dealing with Literature and Publications.

We selected the "Online Book Initiative" Gopher and were taken to the actual OBI Gopher menu, from which we selected Ambrose Bierce. That led to a menu offering three or four items by or about Bierce. We selected *The Devil's Dictionary*, and the actual text of the book appeared.

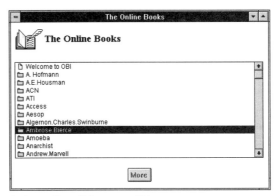

Ambrose "Bitter" Bierce via OBI.

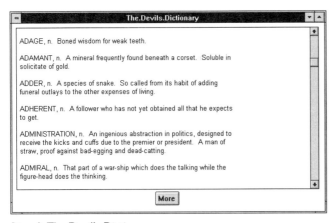

Bierce's The Devil's Dictionary.

Gophering with Your Browser

America Online's Gopher feature is second to none for brand-new users. At this writing, none of the other consumer-oriented online services has done as good a job implementing Gophers.

Trouble is, when you use the AOL Gopher feature, you are pretty much limited to just the subject-specific Gophers the AOL staff has selected for you. That's more than enough at the beginning, but eventually you will want to be able to select your *own* Gopher addresses because you will see them in books like *The Internet Yellow Pages* by Harley Hahn and Rick Stout, and even in this very book.

What to do? The answer is to first check your service to see if there is a way to key in a Gopher address of your own. Failing that, see if

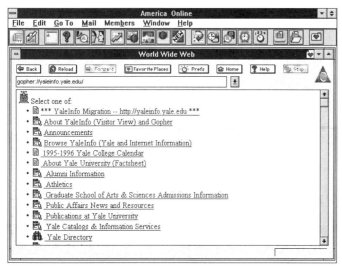

gopher://yaleinfo.yale.edu/

🏛 Select one of:
- 📄 *** YaleInfo Migration -- http://yaleinfo.yale.edu ***
- 🗔 About YaleInfo (Visitor View) and Gopher
- 🗔 Announcements
- 🗔 Browse YaleInfo (Yale and Internet Information)
- 📄 1995-1996 Yale College Calendar
- 📄 About Yale University (Factsheet)
- 🗔 Alumni Information
- 🗔 Athletics
- 🗔 Graduate School of Arts & Sciences Admissions Information
- 🗔 Public Affairs News and Resources
- 🗔 Publications at Yale University
- 🗔 Yale Catalogs & Information Services
- 🔍 Yale Directory

The YaleInfo Gopher via AOL's Web browser.

you can't use your Web browser to tap the Gopher of your choice.

Let's say, for example, that we want to access the Gopher at **yaleinfo.yale.edu**. That's an address we found in *The Internet Yellow Pages* purely at random. As far as we can tell, it is not among the choices offered by America Online's Gopher feature.

But that's not a problem. Simply activate AOL's Web browser, mouse up to the "Go to" box at the top of the screen, and key in **gopher://yaleinfo.yale.edu**. You will then see the screen for the YaleInfo Gopher. The point is that you can use *any* Web browser program to access *any* Gopher site. Just use **gopher://** followed by the Gopher site address as the URL you key into your browser.

Finding Gopher Sites

The only way to really appreciate Gopher is to plunge in and play with the Gopher of your choice. You will find that any given Gopher—like any novel, movie, or song—is only as good as its creators. Some Gophers are very, very good and some are less than adequate. But all are a help in organizing and presenting Net resources and in making them accessible to you.

Now that you know what they are, you'll find Gopher addresses popping out at you nearly everywhere—in magazine articles, newsletters, and even on Web pages. Fortunately, numerous lists of Gopher resources are available. One of the best is the famous Yanoff List, which is also known as "Special Internet Connections." See page 115 for more on the Yanoff List.

We'll have much more to say about the Yanoff List and similar guides to Internet resources later. But if you're in a hurry, the easiest way to get a copy is to send a short e-mail message to: **inetlist@aug3.augsburg.edu**. This is an e-mail responder that will automatically mail you a copy of the list. Be warned, though—it is nearly 30 pages long!

Getting Files
from the Net (FTP)

15

FTP: A GREAT TOOL FOR
TRANSFERRING FILES

Many of the riches of the Internet are stored in files. Yet most
people, truth to be told, have only the vaguest notion of what
files are and do. So, before we tell you how to get files from the
Internet using the feature called FTP (File Transfer Protocol),
it's probably a good idea to take just a moment to note a few key
points about files in general.

Files are Physical

A file is nothing more than a discrete collection of computer bits. Every
file thus occupies a certain amount of hard disk real estate. Files, in
other words, are quite *physical*.

Each file is designed for a very specific purpose. Program files are
designed to *do* things. Data files are designed to give program files

something to do. A good example of a program file is GWS.EXE, Steven Rimmer's shareware Graphic Workshop program. A data file is a file like SHY-DI.GIF. When you run the program GWS.EXE, you can view the data in SHY-DI.GIF and discover that it forms an image of the Princess of Wales.

Program files can only be used with the operating system they were written for, whether it is DOS/Windows, Macintosh, UNIX, or something else. Data files, on the other hand, can often be used on many different systems. Thus any computer user with a graphics program capable of displaying .GIF files could use the same SHY-DI.GIF data file.

File Names and Compression

Files have names, of course, and in the DOS/Windows "Wintel" world, the name often signals the main characteristic of the file. A file with a name that ends in .EXE or .COM or .BAT is a program file. Files with names ending in .TXT are usually text files, and .DOC means a document file of some sort, probably from Microsoft Word. We already know that .GIF indicates a kind of graphic image file.

File names in the Wintel world can be no longer than 11 characters—a maximum of eight to the left of the "dot" or period and a maximum of three to the right. The 11-character file name is the lowest common denominator on the Net. If you use a Macintosh you can give your files names that are up to 31 characters long; Microsoft Windows 95 allows names up to 255 characters.

We bring this up for two reasons. First, if you're using Windows 3.x and you download a file with a long name, Windows will truncate the name to just 11 characters when it stores the file on your disk. Second, if you are not a Windows 3.x user, then you're probably not used to puzzling out 11-character file names and thus may miss a lot of good stuff uploaded by Windows 3.x users.

Remember, once you've got the right program for your particular computer, you can use almost all the sound, image, video, text, and other data files you find on the Net, regardless of the fact that they were created on a different kind of computer.

Files can also be "compressed" so that they take up less disk space and can be sent over the Internet in less time. Better still, groups of files can be compressed into a single "archive" file. That makes it easy to get, say, the dozen or more files that comprise a software package by downloading a *single* compressed archive file.

This is why it is so important to pay attention to the names of the files you see when using FTP on the Internet. It is a simple fact of

The Right Compression Tool for the Job!

When you encounter a file that ends in the file extension listed in the first column, you will need the compression/decompression program listed in the second column. This is not a comprehensive list, but it does contain the extensions you are most likely to encounter.

All of the necessary programs are available on the Net. Look for them at PC-archive FTP sites like **oak.oakland.edu** or **archive.umich.edu**. Mac users should check **mac.archive.umich.edu** and **sumex-aim.stanford.edu**.

For DOS/Windows Users

File Extension	Name of Required Program
.ARC	ARCE
.ARJ	ARJ
.GZ or **.Z**	GZIP or GUNZIP
.HQX	XBIN
.LZH	LHA
.SIT	UNSTUFF or UNSIT
.TAR	TAR or EXTAR
.UUE	UUEXE (Richard Marks) or NCDC
.Z	GUNZIP, U16, or COMP
.ZIP	PKUNZIP
.ZOO	ZOO

For Macintosh Users

File Extension	Name of Required Program
.ARC	ArcMac
.CPT	Compactor or Compact Pro
.HQX	BinHex or StuffIt Expander
.LZH	MacLHArc
.SIT	StuffIt Lite, StuffIt, or StuffIt Expander
.TAR	UNTAR
.UUE	UUTOOL
.Z	MacCompress
.ZIP	ZipIt, UnZip, or StuffIt Expander
.ZOO	MacBooz

Internet life that there is no single method for preparing compressed archive files.

You may have heard of PKZIP and .ZIP files. Or StuffIt and .SIT files. But there are at least 15 other compression programs used on the Net, and most cannot unpack archives created by the others.

All You Need Are the Right Tools

That's the bad news. The good news is that decompressing archive files is a simple matter once you've got the necessary program. You can tell which program you need by looking at the file extension: .ZIP requires PKUNZIP, .LZH requires LHA, .CPT requires Compactor or Compact Pro, etc.

The programs you need are widely available on the Net via FTP and in the libraries of AOL and CompuServe. You'll also find the DOS/Windows versions all on a single disk in the Glossbrenner's Choice collection listed at the back of this book. The standards on the Macintosh side, StuffIt and its related programs StuffIt Expander and DropStuff, are all readily available on AOL and CompuServe.

> **Decompressing archive files is a simple matter once you've got the necessary program. You can tell which program you need by looking at the file extension.**

Sometimes, if the person who prepared the archive has taken the extra step needed to make it a "self-extracting" archive, you won't need a special tool at all. Such files end in .EXE in the DOS/Windows world or in .SEA in the Macintosh world.

Thus, if you get a file called GOODIES-Z.EXE and are told that it is a self-extracting archive, all you have to do is click on the file name to "run" the program. The files it contains will be unpacked automatically.

How to FTP—"Anonymously" and Otherwise

FTP is often called "anonymous FTP" because anyone can log on to an FTP site without first establishing an account on that system. When the site prompts you for a user ID, you specify "anonymous." Should you then be asked for a password, you can just key in your e-mail address.

If you're on AOL, you can use that system's built-in FTP feature. If you're not, your best bet is to load your Web browser and specify an FTP URL (the FTP site address preceded by **ftp://**). Your Web browser will automatically handle the details and shield you from the complexities of raw, text-based FTP.

The Key FTP Concept

The key concept to bear in mind is "disk directory path."

This is neither a Wintel nor a Macintosh concept. It is the technique used by the UNIX operating system that Wintel and Mac users must accept at most sites.

Under this system, disk directories and subdirectories are a means of organizing files. FTPing to a location is like loading the Windows File Manager and starting at the top directory on your Wintel computer. The Macintosh analogy is traveling to "folders within folders."

> **To get to a particular file at an FTP site, you have to follow a "path" down the directory "tree" until you reach the subdirectory (or "folder") that holds the file.**

In any event, to get to a particular file at an FTP site, you have to follow a "path" down the directory "tree" until you reach the subdirectory (or "folder") that holds the file. That's why when you're told about an FTP resource, you are usually given both a site address and a path. For example, you might be told that for information on scouting, you can FTP to **ftp.ethz.ch** and follow the path **/rec.scouting/**.

Back to the Books!

We pointed the Netscape browser at the URL **ftp://ftp.std.com**. A nice welcoming message appeared, followed by the beginning of a disk directory. One of the items that showed up as we scrolled down was our old friend from Chapter 14, a directory labeled "OBI," which we know as the Online Book Initiative.

We clicked on that to move down into that directory and saw

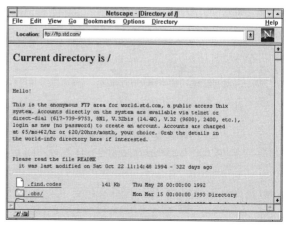

Welcome to the world via FTP!

the screen for the Online Book Initiative. Notice the file "00README." If you click on that file name, a friendly message from Barry Shein of OBI appears, explaining what OBI is all about and urging you to "help yourself" to its files.

You will often encounter "readme" files and their like at FTP sites. And usually it's a good idea to look at them. They can save you a lot of time by telling you how the site is organized and where to look for what. Also notice that moving around is no problem with a browser. You can click on Go and then opt to go back a page. Or you can click on the Netscape line "Up to higher level directory" that appears at the beginning of each subdirectory page.

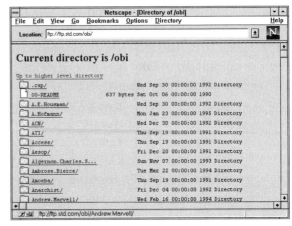

Here's the Online Book Initiative again.

Huckleberry Finn Online

The OBI directory contains a subdirectory for Ambrose Bierce, as you'll recall. But this time we clicked on "Samuel Clemens." We moved down to that subdirectory, and the screen of works by Samuel Clemens appeared.

Notice what the Location box says here. If you guessed that

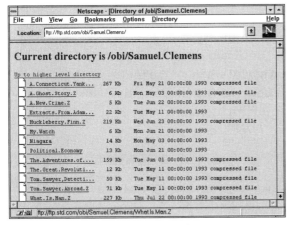

Works by Samuel Clemens (Mark Twain).

we could FTP *directly* to this place by pointing our browser at **ftp://ftp.std.com/obi/Samuel.Clemens/**, you would be absolutely right! That way we would not have to work our way along the directory tree to get here. What's more, with Netscape and other browsers, we can add this specific location to our Bookmarks or Hotlist so we never have to key it in by hand.

File Name Truncation and Decompression

Now, look at the entry called "Huckleberry.Finn.Z." Notice that it is 219KB (kilobytes) long and that it is identified as a compressed file. The extension is .Z, so you consult the chart in this chapter and learn that you're going to need GUNZIP, U16, or COMP or MacCompress, if you're a Mac user, to decompress it. We'll assume that you have GUNZIP.EXE on your hard disk.

So you simply click on the file name. And, after you tell Netscape that you do not want to use a viewer program for this file type, the download begins. You can tell your browser where you want to put the file and what name you want to use for storing it on your disk. If you don't specify a name, the file name will be automatically truncated to HUCKLEBE.Z on DOS/Windows systems.

If you are a truly new Wintel computer user, follow these steps: Once you're offline, make a directory on your hard disk called "Junk." Copy GUNZIP.EXE and HUCKLEBE.Z (or whatever) into it. Go to that directory and key in **GUNZIP HUCKLEBE.Z**. The GUNZIP program will decompress the file into the plain-text original, and it will delete the compressed file to save disk space. That's all there is to it.

If you're a Macintosh user, load MacCompress or the commercial product StuffIt Deluxe if you have it, and tell it to do its thing on HUCKLEBE.Z.

Conclusion: Good FTP Sites

We're real fans of FTP. Certainly, you will encounter Gopher menu items that allow you to FTP a file. But a lot depends on the software you use to access a given Gopher. In our experience, for example, the AOL Gopher took us to the Online Book Initiative site, but when we clicked on Bierce's "*The Devil's Dictionary*," it automatically downloaded the file, decompressed it, and displayed it on the screen.

That may be convenient if you want to get a glimpse of the work before opting to download it. But it is very *inconvenient* (because of the one-screen-at-a-time approach AOL uses when you want to capture displayed text) if you go in knowing that you want to have that particular file transferred to your computer.

Gopher menus may well be the best way to explore the Net. But when you want to *download* a file, you may find that FTP is the better tool. As to where you should look for lists of really good FTP sites, we'll save that for the chapters in Part 5. The Yanoff List mentioned in the last chapter, and many other similar resources, contain the addresses of countless topic-specific FTP sites.

Signing On to a
Distant Computer (Telnet)

16

Telnet *is the oldest of all Internet features. And frankly, it is not only showing its age, but it also has been largely relegated to the backwaters of the Net as everyone moves to the World Wide Web. Still, just as there are some places you cannot use a power saw and must therefore be able to use the much cruder handsaw, there are Internet locations not yet accessible via the Web where you must use Telnet.*

The Library of Congress happens to be one of these locations. You can reach the Library of Congress via the Web by specifying the URL **http://lcweb.loc.gov**. Once there, you will see attractive graphics and lots of hot links on your screen. But when you opt to search for books of interest, you will be "Telnetted" to a location, and your screen will

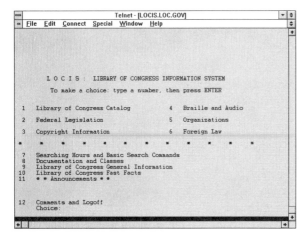

```
 ═                   Telnet - [LOCIS.LOC.GOV]              ▼ ▲
 ═  File   Edit   Connect   Special   Window   Help           ▲
                                                              ▲

        L O C I S :  LIBRARY OF CONGRESS INFORMATION SYSTEM

          To make a choice: type a number, then press ENTER

    1   Library of Congress Catalog        4   Braille and Audio

    2   Federal Legislation                5   Organizations

    3   Copyright Information              6   Foreign Law

    *     *     *     *     *     *     *     *     *     *

    7   Searching Hours and Basic Search Commands
    8   Documentation and Classes
    9   Library of Congress General Information
   10   Library of Congress Fast Facts
   11   * * Announcements * *


   12   Comments and Logoff
        Choice:
                                                              ▲
 ◄ │                                                      │ ►
```

Telnet usually means text.

look like the one shown here. To which you can be forgiven for responding "Ugh!"

Telnet Essentials

You can use your Web browser to Telnet to an address by specifying the URL prefix **telnet://** and following it with the target address. All Telnet really does is establish a connection between your system and the host system at the remote location, just as your favorite communications program establishes a connection between you and CompuServe, AOL, Prodigy, or a local bulletin board system.

As we have said before, what happens next—what happens after the connection has been made—is entirely up to the software that is running on the host system.

For example, if you were to Telnet to a Gopher site, the Gopher program at that site would begin to run and you would see a Gopher menu. If you were to Telnet to a library location, you could expect its card catalogue searching software to begin to run.

But what you'll see when you Telnet will be *plain text*. You won't see the kind of graphical icons and buttons that appear when you use a Gopher URL (**gopher://** followed by a site address), even if you have Telnetted to the same site you have "Gophered" to many times before.

Sign-ons and Port Addresses

Just as you or your software must specify a user name and a password when logging on to one of the Big Three, it is not uncommon for a Telnet site to require a user name of some sort. That's why when you see Telnet sites listed in books and directories, you may see a phrase like "Log on as 'public'" or "Login: guest" or something else.

You may also see that some Telnet addresses end in what's called a "port address." For example, you might be told to Telnet to an address like **downwind.sprl.umich.edu 3000** or to **wind.atmos.uah.edu 3000** to get

U.S. and Canadian weather forecasts, ski conditions, earthquake reports, severe-weather reports, hurricane advisories, and so on.

The "3000" is a port address. The technicalities don't matter—you can think of any numbers following a Telnet site address as merely a part of the address. The only difference is that you leave a space instead of entering the more usual period (.) separator.

Terminal Type?

Once you're into the target system, you may be asked to tell it your "terminal type." If you access a Telnet site using a Web browser, you probably won't have to worry about terminal type.

But you will definitely find inconsistencies at Telnet sites on whether you should hit your Enter key after typing a command. Some systems respond the moment you enter the number you want from a menu. Others will sit forever after you have made your selection, waiting for you to press your Enter key.

For the record, the terminal type that is used on most systems connected to the Internet—and the one that has become the *de facto* standard—is the Digital Equipment Corporation (DEC) VT-100. When you Telnet to most sites, the remote computer will expect you to behave like—to emulate—a VT-100 terminal.

Conclusion: Avoid Telnet If You Can!

Telnet is a relic of Internet history. Your co-authors have never been suckers for the pretty pictures of a graphical user interface. So it's not the text of Telnet connections that makes us say that Telnet is an absolutely *terrible* way to use the Internet. Instead, it is the decades-old "terminal emulation" approach that Telnet takes.

The DEC VT-100, not to mention the IBM 3270, hasn't been the lowest common denominator in many years, and it never *was* that among personal computer users. The only reason for putting up with the burdens Telnet imposes is if you cannot access the site or get the information any other way.

In short, you've still got to know about Telnet, but as time goes on and even the Library of Congress eventually moves completely onto the Web, you will hear less and less about this ancient feature.

Power Searching!

17

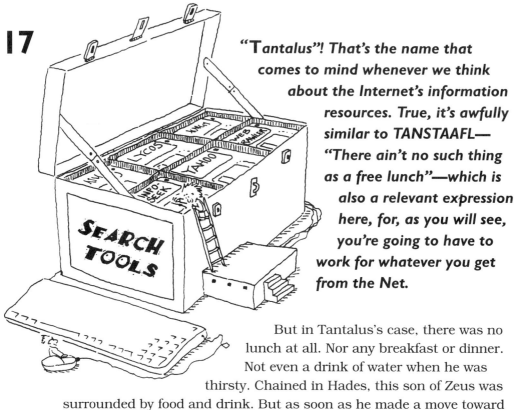

"Tantalus"! That's the name that comes to mind whenever we think about the Internet's information resources. True, it's awfully similar to TANSTAAFL— "There ain't no such thing as a free lunch"—which is also a relevant expression here, for, as you will see, you're going to have to work for whatever you get from the Net.

But in Tantalus's case, there was no lunch at all. Nor any breakfast or dinner. Not even a drink of water when he was thirsty. Chained in Hades, this son of Zeus was surrounded by food and drink. But as soon as he made a move toward it, it would move away, just out of reach.

Approaches to the Problem of "Information"

Although they don't jump out of reach as you approach, the information resources available over the Internet are just as tantalizing, but for a different reason. You know the answer to your question is there—just a few keystrokes away—but *where*? What feature should you tap? What *keys* should you tap? That's the challenge we'll address in this chapter and in the other chapters in this part of the book.

Longtime Internauts have been grappling with the problem from the beginning, decades before the explosion of Internet subscribers and sites that began in the early 1990s. One technique that has worked fairly well was to create lists of resources. As we'll see in later chapters, there are topic-specific lists, and lists of the "best" features of any sort on the Net.

The entire Gopher system was obviously designed to make it easier for users to find the information they need. There are also features that search collections of Gopher menus for what you want. And there are Gophers that have been specifically designed to focus on the Net as a whole, instead of just the resources available at a single university or other location.

Most exciting of all, in recent years—years? heck, *months*!—a clutch of automated, interactive searching features has appeared. These are very powerful and very easy to use, which is to say, they are really, really neat. In our opinion, this is where you should start on your quest to find information on the Net.

Start Your Search Engines!

If you use Netscape to access the Web, you have almost certainly visited the Netscape home page (**http://home.netscape.com**). That's because the Netscape program is set to take you there by default each time you use it. (You can change that setting, of course.)

Among the things you will find on the Netscape home page is a feature called "Exploring the Net." Click on it and you'll soon see a page with headings like "Net Search" and "Net Directory." Among the "search engines" you can select are Alta Vista, DejaNews Research Service, Excite, Infoseek, Lycos, WebCrawler, and Yahoo!. For detailed information on the approach each search engine takes, click on "Net Search" or just point your browser at **http://home.netscape.com/escapes/internet_search.html**.

The Reviews Have Begun

Technically, a search engine is the piece of software used to actually conduct a database search. It's not the term we would use to describe features like Lycos and Infoseek (we'd probably just call them "search tools"). But it really does get to the heart of the matter.

You know how different word processing, spreadsheet, and paint programs vary in their capabilities, their ease of use, and their general layout and design? Well, the same applies to search engines. Each has its own way of doing things.

Fortunately, *PC Computing*, *Internet Magazine*, and other publications have begun to do in-depth reviews of such features. And we were pleased to find that the reviews confirm our own unscientific opinions—Infoseek and Yahoo! are among the top-rated tools on everyone's list. So those are the two we'll focus on here.

Key Questions and Concepts

Your co-authors have written a lot about online searching over the last 15 years, and if there's one thing we know, it is that successful searching is a skill that requires the active engagement of your brain. You've got to think! In fact, you've got to do more than that—you've got to *out-think* the database you're searching.

Try to think of the most unique word, phrase, or name that you would logically expect to find in any discussion of your target topic. Then use that as your search term.

Searching is a book-length topic, so if you want to learn more, see *Online Resources for Business* (John Wiley & Sons, 1995). This is a complete update of our 1986 book *How to Look It Up Online.* Here we have room for but one tip: Try to think of the most unique word, phrase, or name that you would logically expect to find in any discussion of your target topic. Then use that as your search term.

It is also important to pay close attention to just what is being searched—and "when." If you use Infoseek Guide, for example, you can "search and browse Web pages, Usenet newsgroups, FTP and Gopher sites, and more" free of charge. But the Infoseek Guide service does not cover *all* newsgroups, and the database of newsgroups it searches does not date back more than a few weeks.

Trust No One!

It is crucial to be aware that, just because it's online doesn't mean it is accurate or true. In general, you should trust what you find on the Internet even less than you trust what appears in your favorite newspaper or on the evening news.

To say nothing of what you read in *Time* magazine, which may never recover from the fiasco of its July 3, 1995, "cyberporn" cover story. Written by Phillip Elmer-DeWitt, the article claimed to be based on a "Carnegie Mellon study"—which turned out to be nothing more than a poorly researched undergraduate paper. (To read the article, go to **http://www.pathfinder.com**.)

The point is that if a news-gathering organization like *Time* can be taken in, what chance does the average person have when facing the flood of "information" on the Net? That's why we say you should be skeptical of everything!

DejaNews, on the other hand, does claim to search nearly a year's worth of newsgroup postings and articles. But DejaNews does not cover every Internet newsgroup either. At least not at this writing.

"Comprehensive" or Not?

Still, even if you could search all available newsgroup postings for the past 12 months, you wouldn't be searching "everything." What about all items on all the Gopher menus in the world, a collection of information Internauts call "Gopherspace?" What about all the files located at FTP sites around the globe? And how about all the interesting Telnet locations and mailing lists?

There are times when it is important to conduct as wide-ranging and comprehensive a search as you can—like, oh, when your job depends on it—and there are times when all you want is a quick answer. The important thing is to be aware that there's a difference between a quick search and a comprehensive search, and to pick the one that's right for your current need.

Infoseek: Top of the List

To reach the Infoseek home page, point your browser at **http://guide.infoseek.com**. When the page appears, click on "Search the Web for FREE!"

The Infoseek search page will appear. Since Oriental rugs are a hobby of ours, we decided to see what information and features the Net had to offer in this area. So we keyed in "oriental rugs" as our search term.

Using Infoseek to query the World Wide Web.

Notice that we included the quotation marks in the search to tell Infoseek that we wanted it to treat those words as a phrase. You will find many other tricks and a great deal of good advice if you click on "Helpful Tips" on the Infoseek page. But we strongly advise you to get in there and play for a while before bearing down on the particulars.

Within seconds, Infoseek presented us with a screen of search results. We scrolled down and saw a feature called "Oriental Rug Encyclopedia," and what a find it turned out to be. Pick a carpet type, and a wonderful photo of a representative sample appears on your screen.

Notice that, thanks to the Web, you can click on anything Infoseek finds for you and be taken there immediately. No need

Oriental rugs galore!

Oh, Treacherous Searches

Most Internet search engines deploy special programs called "spiders" that automatically go from Web site to Web site seeking out URLs and page contents. That information is sent back to the spider's home base, and it is this collection of information that gets searched when you use a search engine.

Search engines thus conduct what's called a "full-text" or "free-text" search. That means they look through all the text they have collected for the words you have specified. That sounds great, but in reality this is the crudest of all online searches.

Leave aside the fact that all the "cool" home pages created by every college kid in the country are part of the data that is being searched. Leave aside the duplication and the repetition.

Instead, imagine that you're looking for information about labor unions and strikes in the iron and steel industry. Imagine you tell your search engine to bring you only items that contain all of the following words: "labor," "union," "strike," "iron," and "steel."

So what about this item the search engine retrieved in the curriculum of Stanford University about Romantic poets?

It's a memo from an English professor that includes this sentence: "Friends, we do not labor in vain. We must steel our souls, and have faith in the union of our spirits. We must strike while the iron is hot and see to it that Wordsworth, Coleridge, and Byron are never removed from the curriculum!"

Every word you searched for is in those three sentences—yet the item has absolutely nothing to do with your own topic of interest. In the information business, that's called a "false drop." False drops are what make full-text searches so treacherous.

to remember or key in the Net addresses yourself. When you're done, you can click on Go on the Netscape menu bar, and then click on Back to return to the previous screen. (You'll learn more about using Netscape in the "Web Browser Cookbook" section at the end of this book.)

More and More with Infoseek

We think Infoseek will blow you away—it really is that good! But you should definitely try other services and search engines as well. This is a rapidly evolving field, and it may well be that some other search engine will better suit your needs.

Nor should you necessarily expect all search engines to be available free of charge. Again, policies and business plans are rapidly evolving. For example, Infoseek began by offering everyone the opportunity to

---

This might not be a problem if you have all the time in the world and if all your "transactions" are free. But false drops are a huge problem for anyone hoping to use the Internet to quickly and cheaply locate truly valuable information.

What's the alternative? If you want to be able to go online and say something like, "Give me a list of every company in the vending machine business that is listed on a stock exchange and had earnings of more than $27 per share last year," you are probably not going to be able to find the information—for free—on the Internet.

Why? Because the only way you can do such a precise search is if someone has paid a bunch of people to type that kind of information into a database program. In a real database, every piece of information, whether it is the first name of the company president or the zip code of the plant in Sacramento, has been plugged into its own separate "field."

So a searcher can say: Give me the name and phone number of every company where the field "city" is "Cleveland" and the field "state" is "OH," and the field "gross revenues" is "$5 million or more."

You can use an Internet search engine to look for the words "Cleveland," "OH," and "$5 million." But what if the item of information you want uses "five million dollars" or "$5,000,000" instead of "$5 million"? What if it uses "Ohio" instead of "OH"? The answer is that in those cases, the search engine will not find it.

Some Internet search engines claim to have special techniques for overcoming limitations like these. But in our experience, if you need that kind of precision, your best bet is to contact the reference librarian at a good library or hire a professional searcher. The nonprofit Association of Independent Information Professionals will tell you how to do just that. Contact them at 212-779-1855 or via e-mail at **73263.34@compuserve.com**.

search Web pages for free. But if you wanted to also search postings to newsgroups, you had to pay a monthly fee. Due to competition from services like DejaNews, that policy lasted less than 12 months.

Now Infoseek offers two services: Guide and Professional. Infoseek Guide can be used to search Web pages, newsgroups, FTP sites, Gopherspace, and more, free of charge. Infoseek Professional lets you search all of those items, plus professional newsletters, newswires, magazines, trade journals, and similar "premium" publications.

A subscription to Infoseek Professional is $4.95 per month for 50 "transactions." (A transaction is an online search or a document retrieval.) Subsequent transactions are billed at a dime apiece. But is it worth it?

Yes! But not for the reasons you may assume. The reason your co-authors are happy to pay the $4.95 per month is that the free Infoseek Guide service is usually overcrowded and slow. We don't use Infoseek Professional to search premium publications but to search Web pages, newsgroups, and the like.

Yahoo!: Well, All Right!

We love the attitude and the "voice" that comes through in Infoseek's explanatory text and files. And we feel the same way about Yahoo!. In

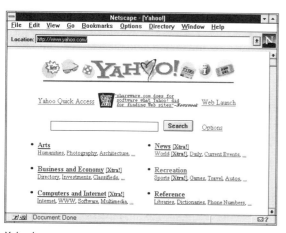

Yahoo!

both cases, you get a sense of incredible competence combined with boundless joy and enthusiasm.

When you point your browser at **http://www.yahoo.com**, you are sure to get solid encouragement to just "pick a subject and dive in." You can search the Yahoo! data-base in much the same way that you can search Infoseek. But we decided instead to "dive" by click-ing on "Recreation." That led to a menu offering topics like "Animals," "Automobiles," "Aviation," "Cooking," "Dating," "Fashion," "Games," "Hobbies and Crafts," and "Travel."

We clicked on "Cooking." What then appeared was a two-and-a-half-page list of clickable items ranging from "The Alaska Seafood Cookbook" to "Chili," from a clutch of recipe archive locations to "Strawberry Facts," and from the "Beer Page" to all kinds of stuff about vegetarianism.

We clicked on "Ancient Rome," and got a collection of ancient Roman recipes. Recipes from an ancient Roman cookbook! Is that cool or what?

Recipes from ancient Rome!

Conclusion

We are just emerging from the stage on the Internet that is equivalent to the Oklahoma Land Rush of 1889. The wagons, horses, and people were lined up; a shot was fired; and the race to stake a claim was on. Countless numbers of claims were staked.

So now what? Now we begin the process of building roads, installing road signs, and creating maps. Because, after all, what good does it do anyone to be on the Internet if no one can find you?

Infoseek and Yahoo! are among the best, but they are not the last word in this area. As we said at the beginning of this chapter, you will find it very convenient to go to the Netscape location **http://home.netscape.com/escapes/internet_search.html**. Once there, search engines like Excite, Alta Vista, and Magellan, as well as Yahoo! and Infoseek, are just a mouse click away.

Finally, once you've had some hands-on experience, you may be ready for the ultimate in Internet searching power (at least at this writing). You may be ready for WebCompass from Quarterdeck Select. Although you can run it with less, you really should have a Pentium system with at least 16 megabytes of RAM, a CD-ROM drive, and 40 megabytes of free hard disk space. The street price is about $100.

WebCompasss is a program that can be told to simultaneously search Yahoo!, Infoseek, Lycos, and all the other search engines you care to specify. Once the program finds what you're looking for, it compiles and lists all relevant documents, eliminates duplicate hits, and, at your option, generates an abstract of each document.

WebCompass catalogues the abstracts and site addresses, and organizes everything into personal indexes, customized to your needs. The package comes with a topic database containing over 40,000 entries to get you started. For more information, call 800-683-6696, extension 6873. Or visit the company's Web site at **http://www.qdeck.com**.

Gopher, Veronica, and Jughead

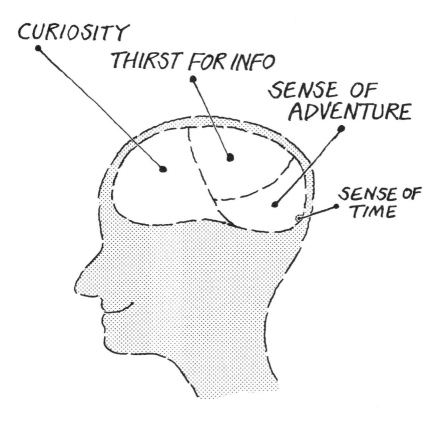

WEB USER'S BRAIN

18

CURIOSITY

THIRST FOR INFO

SENSE OF ADVENTURE

SENSE OF TIME

We love *power searching of the sort discussed in the previous chapter. Yet the Web pages and newsgroups that the leading search engines cover are only part of the story. There is also Gopher. As you may remember from Chapter 7, "Gopher" is the Internet feature designed to make it easy to create a menu system of links to Internet resources.*

In all the excitement about the Web, people have lost sight of Gopher. Some Gopher locations haven't been updated in over a year, while others have been shut down completely. This is a huge mistake, for

Gopher is clearly one of the best features on the Net. And it is still one of the best information retrieval features—Yahoo!, WebCrawler, and Infoseek notwithstanding!

Making Any Internet Feature Accessible

In the first place, unlike most search engines, Gopher menus are *subject-driven*. Their creators don't care whether a given piece of information is available as a Web page, a newsgroup article, an "FTPable" file, a Telnet site, or anything else. The key question is always "Is this resource relevant to the topic, and is it good enough to merit inclusion?"

Second, human beings are asking the questions. That means that the only way any item can appear on a Gopher menu is if a real, live human being looked at the item and decided to create a menu item that would point to it.

This is worth thinking about. Imagine, for example, that you're planning a trip to Venice. You would probably start by checking the Web and one or more of the search engines discussed in Chapter 17.

So you do a search and come up with several hundred hits, which you begin to explore. After a while you discover that one heck of a lot of the hits are Web pages created by high school and college students and by senior citizens to recount their recent trips to Venice. Nothing wrong with that.

The human filter that Gopher brings to bear is simply invaluable.

But you were looking for more detailed information on Venetian museums, their holdings, when they are open, recommended hotels, restaurants and cafes, prices, and how much to tip a gondolier. You don't want a personal journal or a report on "How I Spent My Summer Vacation" but some really good travel information!

The relevant reports, facts, figures, and phone numbers may well exist on the Web pages your search engine brings you, but who has time to look at all of those hundreds of pages?

The Gopher Approach

Now consider the Gopher approach. Imagine that some bright, Internet-savvy person somewhere decides to create a menu system that will make it easy for you to select and use Net resources of any kind that deal with Venice. He or she explores the Net and the Web, Telnet sites, FTPable files, newsgroups, mailing lists, and the like, and says, "Yep, that's a good one. Nope, that feature is not up to snuff. Oh, and I've got to include this one . . ."

The result is a menu of Venice-related Internet features that some man, woman, or committee has looked at and judged to be worthy, arranged in an easy-to-use format. There might be a menu item reading "Venetian Restaurants," for example. Click on it, and you'll be taken to a submenu containing selections like "Cheap," "Moderately Priced," and "Expensive." Click on one of those, and you might be presented with a list of restaurants. And so on.

The human filter that Gopher brings to bear is simply invaluable. The downside is that there may not be a Gopher menu—or items on any Gopher menu anywhere—that address your particular concern or interest. But then, the same could be said of the current collection of World Wide Web pages.

The Best Way to Use Gopher: Veronica!

One drawback to the Gopher approach is that you've got to work your way through a series of nested menus to get to what you want. Fortunately, a Net feature called Jughead will let you *search* the text of all of the menu items, or "titles" as they are sometimes called, in a single Gopher.

There is also the fact that Gophers tend to be subject-specific. That's great when you know that a Gopher devoted to, say, Italy, exists and that it probably contains information on Venice. As long as you know the URL to key in to reach it, you're in business. But what if you don't know which of the 5,000 Gopher servers is likely to be devoted to your subject of interest? Then you consult a feature called Veronica.

It All Began with Archie

Here's what to do. point your browser at **http://www.yahoo.com/Computers_and_Internet/Searching_the_Net**. Notice that Yahoo! offers you four selections, including not only Jughead and Veronica, but also Archie.

The whole comic-strip-character thing on the Internet started with Archie, a name derived from "archive," as in "file archive." Archie lets you search for files available via FTP. Unfortunately, you can only search by file name, so if you don't have some idea of what the file's called, you're probably out of luck.

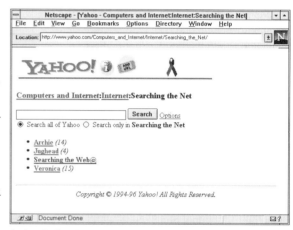

Archie, Jughead, and Veronica via Yahoo!

Using Veronica

So what's Veronica? Veronica is a search engine designed to search all the Gophers in the world. Click on Veronica, and you'll see a screen like this one. Click on one of the "Veronica Server" selections, and you'll be taken to a screen where you can type in the keyword you want to search on.

We keyed in the word "peppers" at that point and were rewarded with a screen like the one shown at the top of the next page. Notice that we've got files, articles, and even graphic images in .GIF, .PCX, and .TIFF formats. And this is only a small portion of what Veronica found for us.

And notice that every item on the screen contains the word "peppers." Veronica has essentially created an instant Gopher menu devoted to the topic of peppers.

The technical details aren't important. But basically, Veronica servers have "harvester" programs that are similar to the "spider"

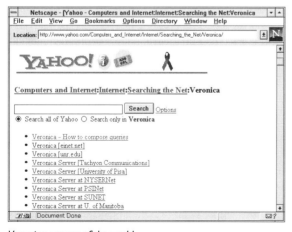

Veronica servers of the world.

programs Infoseek, WebCrawler, and other search engines use to collect information about World Wide Web sites. The harvesters periodically visit nearly every Gopher site in the world and collect their contents.

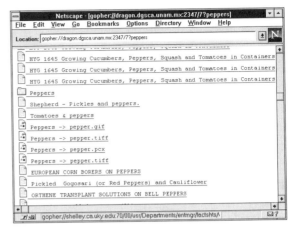

Veronica delivers: peppers galore!

Those contents consist of the menu item title and the link or pointer information attached to it. This gets pumped back to the Veronica server, where it is combined with other harvestings to create a gigantic (over 15 million items) database of Gopher menu item titles. It is this database that is searched when you use Veronica. This database is sometimes referred to as "Gopherspace."

Conclusion

Finally, there are two features we really like about Veronica. First, Veronica will give you all of your hits at once. Infoseek, Yahoo!, and the others deliver hits in batches of 10, 25, or some other number you may be able to specify. Of course, they have to do this because their searches often turn up hundreds of items.

Second, Veronica offers some very powerful features not available on most Web search engines. These features are explained in the text file that will appear when you click on "Veronica—How to compose queries" in Figure 18-2. But, briefly, in addition to being able to use "and," "or," "not," and wildcards (*), you can also limit your search to just certain types of resources. Thus, you can tell Veronica that you want just sound files or just .GIF image files, and so on.

The vast stores of information and other resources available via the Net and the Web are useless if you can't find what you need quickly and easily. In our opinion, search engines of the sort discussed in the previous chapter are only part of the solution. The other part may just lie with Gopher and Veronica.

Finding and *Searching* Newsgroups of Interest

19

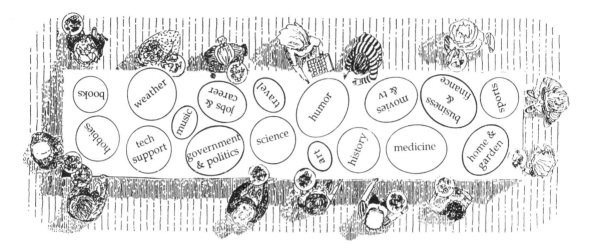

Over 20 years ago a remarkable series of books began to appear whose main purpose was to capture the folk wisdom of the people who live in the "hollers" of West Virginia and similar locations. These were the famous Foxfire books, of course. They come to mind now because folk wisdom and shared personal experience is very much the essence of Internet newsgroups.

In some respects, we, you, and everyone else are likely to find this kind of information far more useful in our daily lives than the more formal, traditional kinds of information held by books, magazines, newspapers, and special reports. The trouble is, with more than 15,000 newsgroups to choose from, how do you find the one you need and want? And how do you find the answers to your questions?

There are two solutions. Both are valid, recommended, and in no way mutually exclusive. The first is to get a list containing the names and brief descriptions of all existing newsgroups and use the "find" function of your word processor to search for what you want. The second is to go online and do a "power search" of the actual contents—the messages people have posted—of various groups.

The Lawrence List Approach

One thing you will quickly learn about the Net is that there is a FAQ file for nearly everything. In the case of newsgroups, the FAQ is called Answers to Frequently Asked Questions about Usenet, and it is posted regularly to the newsgroups **news.announce.newusers** and **news.answers**.

What is generally considered the most authoritative list of newsgroups was created by Gene Spafford and then taken on by David C. Lawrence. The list is organized into two broad categories. There are the

A Snippet of the Lawrence List

Here is just the tiniest snippet of the Lawrence list of Internet newsgroups. We have picked the recreational portion, but we have deleted scores and scores of groups in order to cut things down to displayable size. So please view the list that follows as but a mere sampling.

```
-----------------------------------------------------------------
Newsgroup                Description
-----------------------------------------------------------------
rec.animals.wildlife     Wildlife-related discussions and information
rec.antiques             Discussions of antiques and vintage items
rec.aquaria              Keeping fish and aquaria as a hobby
rec.arts.bodyart         Tattoos and body-decoration discussions
rec.arts.bonsai          Dwarfish trees and shrubbery
rec.arts.books.tolkien   The works of J. R. R. Tolkien
rec.arts.cinema          Discussion of the art of cinema (moderated)
rec.arts.sf.misc         Science fiction lovers' newsgroup
rec.arts.tv.soaps.abc    Soap operas produced by or for the ABC network
rec.arts.wobegon         "A Prairie Home Companion" radio show discussion
rec.aviation.stories     Anecdotes of flight experiences (moderated)
rec.aviation.student     Learning to fly
rec.birds                Hobbyists interested in bird watching
rec.boats.building       Boat building, design, restoration, and repair
rec.climbing             Climbing techniques, competition announcements, etc.
rec.collecting.stamps    Discussion of all things related to philately
rec.crafts.winemaking    The tasteful art of making wine
rec.food.cooking         Food, cooking, cookbooks, and recipes
rec.food.drink           Wines and spirits
rec.food.drink.beer      All things beer
rec.food.drink.coffee    The making and drinking of coffee
rec.music.ragtime        Ragtime and related music styles
rec.scuba                Hobbyists interested in scuba diving
```

Alternative Newsgroup Hierarchies (all the alt. groups) and the List of Active Newsgroups (comp., rec., sci., and everything else).

Each of these categories is further divided into several files. As a convenience to our readers, we've collected all of the files and made them available on the Newsgroup Essentials disk available from Glossbrenner's Choice. But you can get them yourself online via FTP or newsgroup postings. Once you get the lists on your disk, use your word processor to do a keyword search for items of interest. Here are some of the places to look online for the files of the Lawrence list:

- FTP to **ftp.uu.net**
  Path: **/usenet/news.answers/alt-hierarchies/part***
  Path: **/usenet/news.answers/active-newsgroups/part***

- Check these newsgroups:
  news.lists
  news.groups
  news.announce.newgroups
  news.answers

Searching Newsgroups with DejaNews

As you may remember from Chapter 17, Infoseek lets you search its database of Web pages and newsgroups. But it makes no claim of offering a complete archive of newsgroup postings. That's where DejaNews comes in.

You can reach this feature by pointing your browser at **http://www.dejanews.com** or you can find it on the main Internet menu offered by America Online.

The name, of course, is a pun on "déjà vu," which literally means "already seen." In lay terms, this is the phrase that describes that sensation you have when you suddenly feel you're reliving a part of your life in real time. "Been there; done that; got the T-shirt" about sums it up.

Well, DejaNews claims to have the largest collection of indexed, archived Usenet news available anywhere. DejaNews gives you access to most of the Usenet postings in the last month.

This is important because, while the length of time a given posting remains "on the system" is up to the system administrator at the site that carries the Usenet news feed, in most cases stuff "scrolls off" (is deleted) after about two weeks. DejaNews has announced plans to make an entire year's worth of newsgroup postings available soon.

Welcome to DejaNews!

The only negative point is that DejaNews does not cover *all* newsgroups. It does not cover any of the alt., soc., or talk. groups, and it does not cover any groups that end with the word "binaries."

Going After the Woodpeckers

Still, DejaNews is free, and it does an absolutely superb job. For example, we love birds, but recently a downy woodpecker has been pounding the hell out of a spot near the roof of our guest cottage.

Is it possible that other Internet users have had similar problems? We went to DejaNews and the home page appeared. We moused around, got to the search window, and searched on "woodpeckers and house and damage."

We were truly amazed. No one we know has ever had a woodpecker problem, so we thought it was unique. Not so at all. Lots of people on the Internet have had the identical problem, and many of them have offered suggestions and solutions. Wow!

A minute or two later, we had the kind of reaction you might have on seeing a ghost. It was absolutely eerie. We did another search, and another, and another. Any topic we could think of—whether it was woodpeckers pounding on the side of the house or squirrels in the

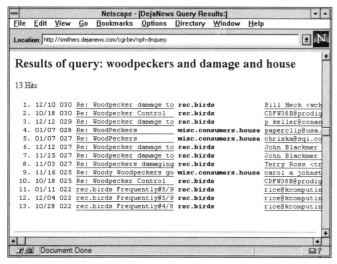

Results of query: woodpeckers and damage and house

13 Hits:

```
 1. 12/10 030 Re: Woodpecker damage to  rec.birds            Bill Heck <wch
 2. 10/18 030 Re: Woodpecker Control     rec.birds            CDFW38B@prodig
 3. 12/12 029 Re: Woodpecker damage to  rec.birds            p_keller@conan
 4. 01/07 028 Re: WoodPeckers            misc.consumers.house paperclip@usa.
 5. 01/07 027 Re: WoodPeckers            misc.consumers.house chriska@sqi.co
 6. 12/12 027 Re: Woodpecker damage to  rec.birds            John Blackmer
 7. 11/25 027 Re: Woodpecker damage to  rec.birds            John Blackmer
 8. 11/03 027 Re: Woodpeckers damaging  rec.birds            Terry Ross <tr
 9. 11/16 025 Re: Woody Woodpeckers go  misc.consumers.house carol a johnst
10. 10/18 025 Re: Woodpecker Control     rec.birds            CDFW38B@prodig
11. 01/11 022 rec.birds Frequently#5/9  rec.birds            rice@kcomputin
12. 12/04 022 rec.birds Frequently#5/9  rec.birds            rice@kcomputin
13. 10/28 022 rec.birds Frequently#4/8  rec.birds            rice@kcomputin
```

What do you do with an overeager woodpecker?

attic—yielded numerous postings offering tips, hints, and advice on how to deal with the problem.

Now *that's* information the average person can use. And Internet newsgroups have tons and tons of it.

And you know what else? The way DejaNews is set up, you can easily get a list of the other messages any given person has posted to any newsgroup. You can send the individual a private e-mail message. Or you can post your own message to the newsgroup in response to someone else's comment.

With the Lawrence list of newsgroups and DejaNews, you will be well on your way toward taking maximum advantage of the resources newsgroups offer.

Free Resource Lists

20

The computer-driven searches offered by Infoseek, Yahoo!, Veronica, and the like are so powerful, so fast, and so fun to use that you may never pause to wonder what people did before these features appeared. And if you did happen to ask that question, you might find yourself answering, "Why should I care?"

The answer to both questions is that for decades, individual Internet users have been creating and maintaining lists of Internet resources, and these lists are still quite important and valuable. (This is done out of the goodness of their hearts, but none would deny that it's kind of fun to have your name associated with an authoritative list of Internet resources.)

None of the search engines we've told you about can give you the comprehensive look at the Net's selection of mailing lists offered by the SRI or PAML lists discussed in Chapter 13. And, the DejaNews feature you learned about in Chapter 19 may be free, but it does not include the alt., soc., or talk. groups, or groups that end in the word "binaries."

Our point is that, while you may want to do power searching most of the time, you still need to consult some of the classic lists prepared by longtime Internauts. The three we think you will want to start with are the Clearinghouse Subject Guides, the Yanoff List, and the Rovers List. All three can be consulted on the Net in their Web versions, but you can also obtain them via FTP.

The Clearinghouse for Subject-Oriented Internet Resource Guides

The University of Michigan's University Library and the School of Information and Library Studies (SILS) have established a system for creating and distributing some truly incredible subject-oriented guides to Internet resources. The full title of this project is given in the headline above. Here we'll just call it the Clearinghouse.

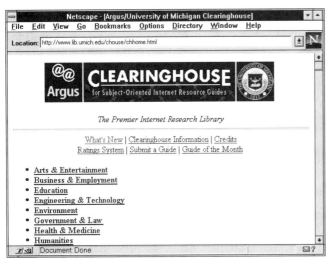

At this writing, nearly 400 guides are available. More are sure to have been added by the time you read this. The guides are prepared by longtime Internauts and by SILS students working under a faculty advisor as part of the Internet Resource Discovery Project.

Welcome to the Clearinghouse!

Although they vary in quality and comprehensiveness, most guides are on the order of 20 pages or more of single-spaced text. And they typically cover *everything* on the Net that pertains to a topic: Gophers, Telnet sites, World Wide Web home pages, files you can FTP, news-groups, mailing lists, bulletin board systems—the works!

How to Get to the Clearinghouse

There are lots of ways to get to the Clearinghouse at the University of Michigan. Perhaps the easiest is to point your Web browser at **http://www.lib.umich.edu/chouse/chhome.html**. That will bring up the Clearinghouse home page.

The list begins with "Arts & Entertainment" and continues on down the line. Click on any of these items, and you will be taken to a subsidiary menu that brings things into sharper focus. For an example, take a look at the Arts & Entertainment page.

Each of the items listed on the screen is a Clearinghouse list of subject-specific Internet resources. Click on an item, and the site will send you a plain text file.

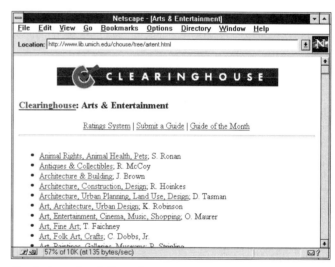

Clearinghouse Arts & Entertainment reports.

The file will appear on your screen. But you will want to save it to disk, so click on File, then Save As, then File Type. Finally, click on Text and specify a name for the file. Netscape or whichever browser you are using will save the information to disk.

Searching the Clearinghouse

This is a great way to browse the Clearinghouse. But you won't want to miss its search function. You will find it at the bottom of the menu that appears when you first enter the site. When you opt to search the files, you will discover that you are doing a Gopher search.

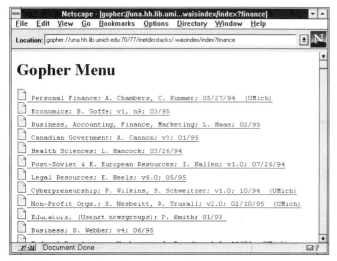

Gopher Menu

Personal Finance; A. Chambers, C. Kummer; 05/27/94   (UMich)

Economics; B. Goffe; v1, n9; 03/95

Business, Accounting, Finance, Marketing; L. Haas; 02/95

Canadian Government; A. Cannon; v3; 01/95

Health Sciences; L. Hancock; 03/26/94

Post-Soviet & E. European Resources; I. Kallen; v1.0; 07/26/94

Legal Resources; E. Heels; v6.0; 05/95

Cyberpreneurship; P. Wilkins, S. Schweitzer; v1.0; 10/94   (UMich)

Non-Profit Orgs.; S. Nesbeitt, R. Truxall; v2.0; 02/10/95   (UMich)

Educators, (Usenet newsgroups); P. Smith; 01/93

Business; S. Webber; v4; 06/95

Document Done

Clearinghouse search results on "finance."

(See how all of the chapters you've read in this book come together! This is no accident.)

We opted to search on the word "finance," and got a menu of results with lots and lots of items. We clicked on the very first item, and that produced a 20-page, single-spaced report covering everything from investments to taxes to credit cards to personal finance software resources available on the Internet.

Other Avenues

You can also reach the Clearinghouse by picking the relevant item off your local Gopher. If your Gopher doesn't have such, use the RiceInfo Gopher (**riceinfo.rice.edu**). Or Gopher to **gopher.lib.umich.edu** and select "What's New and Featured Resources" and then "Clearinghouse . . . ."

Or you can FTP to **una.hh.lib.umich.edu** and select the path **/inetdirsstacks/**. Once you have FTPed to that location, get the file called ".README-FOR-FTP," or look at the directory of files. You will find that the file names are self-explanatory.

Probably, you should try the Web version of the Clearinghouse first. But bear in mind that the feature makes no claim to covering every topic. To get an idea of which topics it does cover, and to thus target your online time more precisely, you may want to get the Clearinghouse subject guide file. This is available at the addresses given above and on disk from Glossbrenner's Choice.

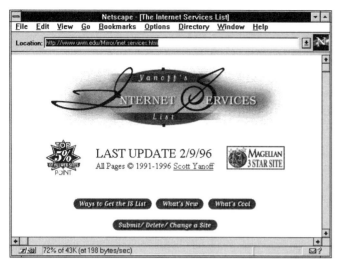

The Yanoff List on the Web.

The Yanoff List

Internaut Scott Yanoff has maintained his list of "Internet Connections" for so many years that it has become known simply as the "Yanoff List." We may be wrong, but our sense of things is that in the early years, the Yanoff List represented a personal view of what was really good and worth checking out on the Net.

These days, it seems to be focused more on classifying Internet resources to make them easier to find, and less on making selections— which is fine and perfectly understandable in light of the explosion of Internet resources in recent years. Our advice: Think of the Yanoff List as the online equivalent of *The Internet Yellow Pages* (an Osborne/McGraw-Hill publication that sells for $30). Its scope is just as breathtaking, and it can be had at almost no cost.

Getting the Yanoff List

The best way to explore the Yanoff List is to point your browser at **http://www.uwm.edu/Mirror/inet.services.html**. Doing so will bring up a very browsable list that will lead you in many interesting directions.

The trouble is, the list is so long that you will have to click on an item and wait as the next part of the list is loaded. That's why we recommend getting the whole thing as a text file. We offer it on disk via Glossbrenner's Choice, but you can go get it yourself by checking the newsgroup **alt.internet.services** or by FTPing to **ftp.csd.uwm.edu**, logging on as "anonymous," and following the path **/pub/inet.services.txt**. Or you can Gopher to **gopher.csd.uwm.edu** and select "Remote Information Services."

We could do an entire chapter on the Yanoff List. But all we have space for here is to urge you to follow our directions for consulting it. You won't be sorry.

The Rovers List of FTP Sites

Finally, Internaut Perry Rovers produces an impressive list of anonymous FTP sites and updates it on a regular basis. For each site, the list tells you which kinds of files and subjects are covered. Put the Rovers List into your word processor and you can search for topics of interest.

Or you can point your browser at **http://www.mid.net/FTP-LIST** to see the list via the Web. This site offers a search option that, while interesting to byteheads like us, is not really ready for prime time. Still, we urge you to check it out.

Here are the FTP sites where Mr. Rovers posts his list. You may also want to pick up his Frequently Asked Questions (FAQ) about the site list. (Look for a file called simply "FAQ" in the directory with the site list.)

- FTP address: **rtfm.mit.edu**
  Path: **/pub/usenet/news.answers/ftp-list/sitelist/**

- FTP address: **ftp.coast.net**
  Path: **/SimTel/msdos/info/ftp-list.zip**

- FTP address: **garbo.uwasa.fi**
  Path: **/pc/doc-net/ftp-list.zip**

- FTP address: **ftp.edu.tw**
  Path: **/documents/networking/guides/ftp-list/**

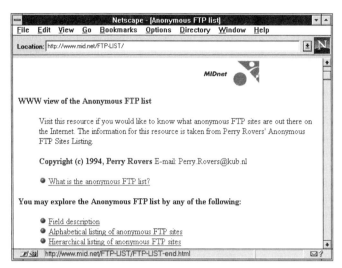

The following is inside the browser window image:

Netscape - [Anonymous FTP list]

File   Edit   View   Go   Bookmarks   Options   Directory   Window   Help

Location: http://www.mid.net/FTP-LIST/

MIDnet

WWW view of the Anonymous FTP list

Visit this resource if you would like to know what anonymous FTP sites are out there on the Internet. The information for this resource is taken from Perry Rovers' Anonymous FTP Sites Listing.

Copyright (c) 1994, Perry Rovers E-mail: Perry.Rovers@kub.nl

● What is the anonymous FTP list?

You may explore the Anonymous FTP list by any of the following:

● Field description
● Alphabetical listing of anonymous FTP sites
● Hierarchical listing of anonymous FTP sites

http://www.mid.net/FTP-LIST/FTP-LIST-end.html

The Rovers List of FTP sites via the Web.

Conclusion

Internet access is rapidly becoming a commodity, with prices settling at around $20 a month for unlimited access via an Internet Service Provider (ISP), or $10 a month for five hours ($3 for each additional hour) via one of the Big Three.

The focus is now moving toward how one *finds information* on the Internet. The chapters in this part of the book have introduced you to many of the leading resources and search engines available to help you find what you want and need on the Net.

The chapters in the *next* part of this book are designed to provide you with really good jumping-off points to various places on the Web related to particular areas of interest. They will show you, in short, how the Internet can fit into nearly every aspect of daily life.

five

The World Wide Web in Your Life

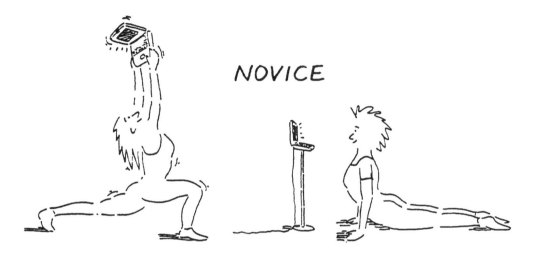

YOGA SURFING

NOVICE

ADVANCED

The World Wide Web
in Your Life

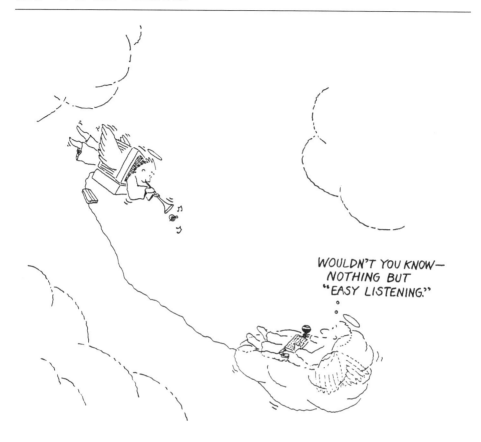

21

WOULDN'T YOU KNOW—
NOTHING BUT
"EASY LISTENING."

On Wednesday, February 7, 1996, Tim Berners-Lee was a guest on the National Public Radio program Fresh Air with Terry Gross. Mr. Berners-Lee is the man who invented the concept of the World Wide Web. (If you'd like a tape of the interview, phone 800-934-6000.)

When asked by Ms. Gross to discuss the origins of the Web, Berners-Lee said that it used to be that "in order to use the ability of the network to move information from one place to another, you had to know all about it.

"What the Web enables you to do is to see information, which is in fact stored on computers which are connected through the network, without being aware of how they are connected or which particular computers are involved. It just allows you to explore the information . . . the Web is the universal space of information."

Ms. Gross then asked Berners-Lee about his frustrations with the Internet before he created the World Wide Web. Berners-Lee replied, "I wouldn't say that I was particularly frustrated with the Internet . . . [but] there was a terrible incompatibility . . . [in] that *almost everything which you needed to know in your daily life* was written down some-where, and at the time, in the 1980s, it was almost certainly written down on a computer somewhere. Somebody had typed it in.

Almost everything you need to know in your daily life is stored in a computer somewhere.

"They had typed it into some computer somewhere. . . . [But] to actually get that information onto your computer would take a lot of knowledge. . . . The whole thing was a mess!" So Mr. Berners-Lee created the Web, and, of course, the folks behind Mosaic and Netscape made the Web graphical by creating Web browser programs.

But you already know all that. What we'd like you to think about here is the Berners-Lee quote that "almost everything which you [need] to know in your daily life" is stored in a computer somewhere and that he created the Web to make it easy for you to find it!

Telling the Truth

Okay. We had already figured out that, yes, the World Wide Web holds information that can be of great use in nearly every aspect of your daily life. In fact, the chapters in this part of the book were written before Tim Berners-Lee did his interview. But to have this fact confirmed by the creator of the World Wide Web himself, and to be told that his main purpose in creating the Web was to make this information easily acces-sible—well, it was too much to resist.

That's why we're so sure that the chapters that follow will excite you. They will show you how the Internet has something to offer for nearly every aspect of your life—whether it is the soul-filling images of the Vatican Exhibition or the mind-filling information you can get on scientific topics from NASA and other sources. All on the Net. All on your computer screen. All in response to the tapping of a few keys or a few mouse clicks.

Here you'll find the keystrokes or mouse clicks you need and the pointers to the right locations. But we must emphasize that the chapters that follow make no pretense of being comprehensive. Think of them instead as some really great starting points for exploring a given topic of interest. For, as we all know by now, on the Net and on the Web, one thing almost always leads to another.

And as cool as the World Wide Web may be, don't forget about Gophers, mailing lists, newsgroups, and all the other Net resources and features you've learned about, as well as the collections of downloadable files available on the Net.

Web sites often pull together and present such resources in a convenient, centralized fashion, so we will concentrate mainly on the Web. But where appropriate, we have also identified relevant newsgroups, Gophers, mailing lists, and the like.

The Net and You—Some Practical Advice

It's entirely possible that at this point you're feeling a bit overwhelmed. It's as if someone has just given you the keys to a high-performance sports car with unlimited mileage and free gasoline. It's almost *too* much.

So stop and take a deep breath. Then admit to yourself that you don't have to locate and sample every Net resource dealing with, say, baseball card collecting. This isn't a contest. It's not a job someone is paying you to do.

Web and Net surfing is *fun!* And you should view it as such. So lighten up and loosen up—and enjoy.

Developing the Online Information Habit

On the other hand, it is certainly true that the Web and the Net can be used for serious, practical information retrieval. But this requires a little time and effort. It also requires you to develop what can be called the "online information habit."

For example, if you've got a dictionary on your shelf, you almost certainly turn to it automatically whenever you encounter an unknown word. Either that, or you decide that discovering the meaning of the word isn't worth the trouble of looking it up. The point is that we all reflexively associate the dictionary with answers to our questions about words.

Developing the online information habit simply means associating the online world with answers to questions about . . . well, about nearly anything. But because this resource is new to you, and because, unlike a dictionary or an encyclopedia, it does not have a physical presence on the bookshelf, you sometimes have to remind yourself to check it.

Maybe we all need a sign above our computers reading "Have you checked the Net today?"

Maybe we all need a sign above our computers reading "Have you checked the Net today?" Whatever. Until we each develop the online information habit, we will never feel the full benefit of the Internet.

Start by Surfing

In our opinion, it is best to start by surfing. Get out there, nose around a bit, see what kinds of things are available. Check the sites and resources profiled in the chapters that follow. Then use the search engines and other features discussed in Chapters 17 through 20 to sharpen your focus.

Ask yourself a question and see if you can find an answer. Just remember that you're never going to locate *all* the files, programs, and resources that concern your particular area of interest. The Internet is far too vast for that. But you will certainly find the major features or sites, because their names will keep coming up again and again.

Information Sophistication

Somewhere in all of our memories is the imprint of what it's like to be a child for whom every experience, every sensation, is exciting and new. For many people today, the Internet and the World Wide Web have rekindled that feeling. And that is marvelous!

But in the years to come, after online access has become as commonplace as wine is now on the American dinner table, people will develop a more discriminating palate. Today, everything looks and tastes good.

It's fun to watch an image of the Mona Lisa appear on your screen, so who cares that there's not much you can do with it once it's there? It's fun to search the Library of Congress card catalogue, despite the fact that you will have to go elsewhere to actually get your hands on any book you find.

In the future, we won't be so wide-eyed. We are likely to say, "Yes, surfing is fun, and I still do it every now and then. But these days I'm much more interested in finding answers to specific questions on the Net and the Web. These days I sign on with a definite purpose in mind!"

Finally, part of becoming sophisticated about information is remembering to be skeptical. Just because someone seems to speak with authority in a newsgroup doesn't mean you should assume that what he or she says is true. Just because a fact or a figure appears on a Web page does not mean that it is accurate. Remember, newspapers and television news shows make mistakes all the time, and they're being *paid* to be conscientious and accurate.

We know you'll have fun exploring the Net. And we hope you will discover that it holds the answers to your questions. So have a blast! Just don't leave your common sense behind.

Art

22

It *is often said, not without cause, that the Internet's resources tend to lean rather heavily toward technology in general and computing in particular. That's why it is nice that by placing things in alphabetical order, we get to start with art.*

In this chapter, we'll look at the WebMuseum Network and the World Art Treasures Web sites. We'll also point you toward a newsgroup and mailing list or two.

The WebMuseum Network: *http://mistral.enst.fr*

The WebMuseum Network is the creation of Nicolas Pioch, who says that his "interests include Latin and Ancient Greek, classical theater, and working on the Internet in my free time, late at night and on weekends." The WebMuseum Network's purpose is to bring to the Net easy access to fine arts information, images, and museum exhibits.

To tap in, point your Web browser at the address given in the subhead above. You will be taken to Paris and shown a screen suggesting that you click on a location geographically closer to you to improve throughput. Since we live on the East Coast, we chose "USA—North Carolina," a site at the University of North Carolina. As an experiment, however, we also clicked on a site in Germany, and the screens and information that appeared were identical to those from the UNC site.

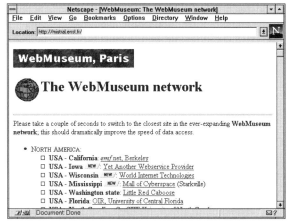

The WebMuseum network.

The purpose of the WebMuseum is to convey information and images related to the art of every age and every culture. A section labeled "Special Exhibitions" included three items when we were there: "Art of the 20th Century," "Cezanne," and "Medieval Art." This last choice took us to "Les tres riches heures du Duc de Berry."

But there were also headings for "Other Resources" and "General Exhibitions." We picked the latter and opted to explore the Web-Museum's famous paintings collection.

Was that ever neat! There was an artist index, a glossary, and a themes index. The themes index began with a list like the one shown here. You can click on any of these items, and be taken to the relevant collection of images and text:

- Gothic Painting (1280–1515)
  - International Gothic Style
  - Innovation in the North
  - Late Gothic Painting

- The Italian Renaissance (1420–1600)
  - The Early Renaissance
  - The High Renaissance

- The Northern Renaissance (1500–1615)

- Baroque (1600–1790)

- Revolution and Restoration (1740–1860)
  - France
  - Germany
  - England
  - Other Countries

- Impressionism (1860–1900)

We opted to go with the artist index, however. A list of artists soon appeared. It included William Blake, Botticelli, Dali, Goya, Raphael, Whistler, and dozens of others. We clicked on Cassatt, Mary. That led to a page that began with an article from the 1994 edition of the *Encyclopedia Britannica* regarding Mary Cassatt, followed by two thumbnail images of her paintings (*Two Women Seated by a Woodland Stream* and *Femme Cousant*).

Click on either thumbnail image, and a screen-size version will be sent to you. Then, if you are using Netscape Navigator, you can click on the image with your right mouse button to pull down a menu that will let you save the image to disk.

Additional Art Resources

If you are interested in a particular painting, artist, or work of art, your best bet is to use one or more of the search engines discussed in Chapter 17. If your interests are more general, two good keyword phrases to try are "fine art" and "art history." We found the Yahoo! site to be particularly rich in links to art-related sites and features.

Other features of interest include the following newsgroups and the Fine Art Forum mailing list:

Newsgroup	Description
humanities.misc	General topics in the arts and humanities.
rec.arts.fine	Fine arts and artists.
alt.binaries.pictures.fine-art.d	Discussion of the fine-art binaries. (Moderated.)
alt.binaries.pictures.fine-art.digitized	Art from conventional media. (Moderated.)
alt.binaries.pictures.fine-art.graphics	Art created on computers. (Moderated.)

Fine Art Forum Mailing List
- Subscription address: **listserv@rutvml.rutgers.edu**
- List address: **fine-art@rutvml.rutgers.edu**

Admittedly, an on-disk image of a famous painting may not have a lot of practical value. But if you have a color ink-jet printer, a printout of such an image can add a nice touch to a kid's garden-variety homework assignment.

World Art Treasures:
http://sgwww.epfl.ch/BERGER/index.html

On the other hand, electronic images of great works of art can be used as the basis for an online course in art history and art appreciation. That's what you'll find at World Art Treasures, a Web site created by the Jacques-Edouard Berger Foundation. Images are drawn from a collection of more than 100,000 slides capturing the art of Europe, Egypt, China, India, and Japan, as well as other civilizations.

Botticelli's Venus.

This is not a database of images, however. It is a collection of presentations of the sort you would find in a college art history course. The text is written by Jacques-Edouard Berger himself, and it is not at all stuffy or pretentious.

We particularly enjoyed the program on Botticelli that explained what's going on in *Birth of Venus* and *Spring*, and pointed out that the two paintings were meant to be displayed side by side. The paintings are shown in thumbnail size, but you can click on them to order up a screen-size image. And, whenever the text mentions a special detail, you can click on it and the site will send you a close-up of that feature.

No one interested in art appreciation should miss this site. It is truly well done.

Books and Authors

23

COOL! BIG PAPER THINGS.

THEY'RE CALLED BOOKS. QUITE POPULAR BEFORE WE HAD INTERNET IMPLANTS.

THIS ONE HAS PICTURES.

MAKE THEM MOVE, DADDY.

The Internet is particularly rich in resources dealing with books and authors. In our experience, these resources fall into at least three categories:

- archive locations that offer the full text of hundreds of great works of literature
- databases like the Library of Congress that can help you prepare a list of publications dealing with a particular topic
- newsgroups and mailing lists devoted to various authors and poets and their works

Fortunately, there are also sites that pull together a large number of topic-specific Net resources and present them as hypertext links on a Web page.

Full Text: Project Gutenberg and the Online Book Initiative

Two of the most important sites offering the full text of great works of literature are Project Gutenberg and the Online Book Initiative. Both rely on volunteers to type the text into files that are then made available for downloading via the Net.

Project Gutenberg was started in 1971 by Michael Hart at the University of Illinois. Hundreds of titles are already available, with thousands more planned by the year 2001. Currently available titles include *Aesop's Fables*, *Alice in Wonderland*, The Bill of Rights, The Book of Mormon, The King James Bible, and *Tom Sawyer*.

To tap into Project Gutenberg, point your Web browser at **http://jg.cso.uiuc.edu/pg/** and then click on "Project Gutenberg Electronic Texts." From there, you can scroll down the list of authors and titles and click on the ones that interest you. (If you expect to use Project Gutenberg a lot, you might want to consider the CD-ROM version. For about $45 you can get all Project Gutenberg files on a single CD-ROM from Walnut Creek CDROM. Call 800-786-9907.)

The Online Book Initiative (OBI) is a creation of Software Tool & Die, and it offers its wares via Gopher. You will find it very easy to use. Point your Web browser at **gopher://world.std.com** and select "OBI The Online Book Initiative." You will see a menu organized mainly by author. When you select a given author, you are taken to a menu listing all of the author's works that are available to you for viewing or downloading.

What's So Great About Full Text?

And just what good is owning the full text of a great work of literature? Certainly no one in their right mind would suggest that you read *Huckleberry Finn* on your computer screen.

No, the real value of this feature lies elsewhere. Over the years we have corresponded with many blind people via electronic mail. These conversations have alerted us to devices that can read text from a computer screen or computer files and convert it into synthesized speech. Thanks to Project Gutenberg and OBI, no unsighted person ever need be deprived of the world's great literature. And downloading the files costs next to nothing.

For sighted people, the main advantage is being able to *search* the work. Remember, novels and other works of fiction are not indexed. So if you're doing a paper on, say, orphan imagery in *Moby Dick*, you can use your word processor to easily search the entire text for every occurrence of words like "orphan," "father," "mother," and so on.

We won't take space here to list all the authors you'll find at OBI. But we do urge anyone interested in obtaining literary works as computer text files to check both Project Gutenberg and OBI.

The Tech Archives from MIT

The Tech is MIT's oldest and largest newspaper. At this writing, it sponsors at least two full-text Web sites—The Shakespeare Homepage and *The Tech* Classics Archive. To tap into either one, point your browser at **http://the-tech.mit.edu** and click on the desired hot link. The Shakespeare home page offers the complete works of the Bard, either one scene at a time or an entire play as one large page, which you must then capture to disk as a file. (If you want an entire play, you may find it more convenient to use OBI or Project Gutenberg.)

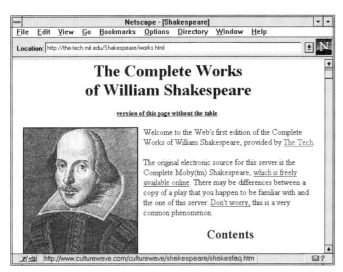

The Shakespeare home page.

The Tech Classics Archive is a searchable archive of 375 classical Greek and Roman texts in English translation. You can search by author, title, date, or translator. Works include Homer's *Iliad* and *Odyssey*, the histories of Herodotus and Thucydides, Virgil's *Aeneid*, and Plato's *Republic*.

Author, Author: *http://www.li.net/~scharf/author.html*

Maria Scharf has created a site called "Author, Author" that currently contains information about what's on the Net regarding nearly 40 authors, including Jane Austen, Allen Ginsberg, Joyce, Keats, H. P. Lovecraft, Twain, Whitman, Wordsworth, and so on.

Different people have created the "pages" for each author. But Eric Lippert's page devoted to J. R. R. Tolkien offers an excellent example. It has a photo of the author, which you can download. It also features a series of categories, each of which has numerous hot links beneath it. These include a list of other Tolkien pages, a list of Tolkien-oriented mailing lists, and a list of Tolkien-oriented newsgroups. Other main categories include "Societies, Conferences, and Newsletters"; "Graphics" (available on the Net); "Online Texts"; and Tolkien parodies.

There's even a link to "The C. S. Lewis Page." Lewis and Tolkien and a fellow named Charles Williams used to meet regularly at Oxford and read aloud their latest works, including, of course, *The Narnia Chronicles* and *The Lord of the Rings*.

Amazon.Com Books: *http://www.amazon.com/*

We discovered Amazon.Com Books through Frederick Zimmerman's Internet Book Information Center (IBIC). (Mr. Zimmerman's IBIC is so extensive that we simply cannot do it justice here. If you are interested in authors and books, however, we strongly urge you to visit this site: **http://sunsite.unc.edu/ibic/IBIC-homepage.html**. You will not be disappointed.)

Publish It Yourself!

Having access to the full text of a work of literature via your computer is great for finding favorite passages. But you know what else? Since all of these works are in the public domain, you can publish them yourself!

Suppose you've got an elderly relative or friend who could benefit from a large-print version of *Alice in Wonderland*. Load that file into your word processing software, select a font of the desired size, and print!

And what about illustrations? Well, we wanted to use something by John Tenniel, the fellow who illustrated *Alice in Wonderland* and *Alice Through the Looking Glass*, for a flyer. We used Infoseek to search on "Tenniel," and we came up with nearly a dozen hits—a dozen locations offering graphics files of the original illustrations.

One of the most impressive locations was at **http://www.cogs.susx.ac.uk/useful/alice/**. It offered all of the Tenniel illustrations for both *Alice* books, thanks to a dedicated individual who took the time and trouble to scan these images into his computer.

We freely admit to having an eerie feeling at this point. This was not a "cooked" example. We had no idea that any Tenniel illustrations would be available. But we knew enough to use Infoseek (or a similar search engine) to check. And, lo and behold, there the images were. It would seem that just about anything you can think of is available on the Net, and that really is amazing.

Still More Sources of Book Information

This wouldn't be a book about the Internet if we didn't mention the Library of Congress. Everyone does. So you should know that you can point your browser at **http://lcweb.loc.gov** or Gopher to **marvel.loc.gov**. It's a nice place to visit and to assemble an impressive list of the books, booklets, pamphlets, etc., that have been published on a given topic in the past two or three hundred years.

But you must remember that the Library of Congress is not a lending library. If you want to get your hands on a copy of a book in its stacks, you'll have to go to Washington, D.C., or search for a library near you that has a copy. (Hint: Ask your local librarian about interlibrary loan programs.)

For in-depth summaries of book-related Internet resources, point your Web browser at **http://www.lib.umich.edu/chouse/chhome.html**. That will take you to the Clearinghouse, a site discussed in Chapter 20. Once you're there, get the following two files: **adultread:allenkrug** and **acadlist.lit**.

There are also nearly 30 newsgroups with "books" in their name. Check the newsgroup hierarchies **rec.arts**, **alt.books**, and **clari.living.books** for groups devoted to children's books, historical fiction, book reviews, Anne Rice's vampire tales, technical books, Tom Clancy, Alvin Toffler, and so forth.

Amazon.Com Books is an online bookstore with a difference. First and foremost, it is an example of a company that has absolutely done it right when it comes to marketing on the Internet. It offers over 1 million titles—more than five times the number you'll find at even the largest "super" bookstore. And it sells all bestsellers for 30 percent off, and all hardcovers and paperbacks for 10 percent off. Shipping within the United States is $3 per order, plus 95 cents per book.

You can search for books of interest on the basis of subject, title, author, or keyword. There's a feature that lets you write your own review of a book for others to read online. And, most impressive of all, there's a feature called "Eyes" that will automatically notify you via e-mail when a given hardcover title comes out in paperback, when a favorite author publishes a new book, or when a book that has been announced finally becomes available.

Computer Help

The Web and Internet probably contain more information about computer hardware and software than any other topic. That makes them incredible resources. But to take advantage of these resources, you need to do two things.

24

First, you've got to flip a switch in your mind that generates the following automatic response, "Got a computer problem? Check online." Second, you've got to learn how to do just that.

The Ruby Slippers of Computer Help

Here's the situation: You've been walking around in a pair of ruby slippers for the last year. They don't go with everything, but, heck, they're comfortable. Now someone comes up and says, "You know, if you just click the heels of those slippers together three times, you will be instantly transported wherever you want to go."

From then on, every time you think "travel," you'll immediately think about your slipper trick. The same is true of your computer questions or problems and the Internet.

The Ultimate Oxymoron: Computer Industry Customer Service

The phrase "computer industry customer service" is very nearly an oxymoron—a contradiction in terms—like "jumbo shrimp." If you don't believe us, pick up the phone and call the company that supplied your computer or created your word processing software.

If you aren't put on "hold" for more than half an hour, take one step forward. If the customer service rep you end up with can actually answer your question, take two steps forward. And if the rep's answers really do solve the problem, advance into the winner's circle and pray you'll be just as fortunate the next time.

The Internet Solution

In our opinion, a call to customer service should be a last resort. Your first response should be to check the Net and possibly the relevant areas of CompuServe, America Online, or Prodigy.

There's a simple reason why these steps are likely to be so productive: Whatever your question or problem, you can bet that tens of thousands of others have experienced it, and you can bet that some of them have addressed it online. In a word, you're not alone. Indeed, you never *were* alone. It's just that the Internet has made it incredibly easy to get together and share information with others.

How to Get Help!

Let's assume you've got a problem. It concerns your Hewlett-Packard (HP) printer, your Hayes-compatible modem, your version of WinFax Pro, Macintosh System 7, DOS 3.3, or something else. Whatever. The bottom line is that something isn't working right. You've checked the manual, and after a frustrating half hour, have decided that the manual's subtitle should be "All hope abandon, ye who enter here!"

Whatever your question or problem, you can bet that tens of thousands of others have experienced it, and you can bet that some of them have addressed it online.

The toll-free customer service number, which you found buried in small type in a footnote on page 86, beckons. Give it a try, but don't give it more than five minutes of being on hold. You can always redial and sit on hold at a later time. Instead, fire up your modem and go online.

The Two Major Types of Online Help

Online sources of computer help information come in two main types: those operated by the hardware or software companies in question, and those that have no such affiliation. Explore both.

Just where should you do your exploring? Your immediate thought might be to start with the Internet. That may well be where you end up, but if you connect to the Net via Prodigy, AOL, or CompuServe, we recommend starting with the Special Interest Groups (SIGs) on those services.

The SIGs offered by the Big Three tend to be very well organized, and the search tools they offer tend to be much more powerful and easy to use than the Internet equivalents. Plus, it costs you no more to use one of the Big Three's SIGs than it does to use one of these services to connect to the Internet. The hourly rate is the same.

If You're a Big Three Subscriber

If you're a Big Three subscriber, sign on and go to your service's "index" or "keyword" feature. On CompuServe, key in **go index**. On AOL, click on the flash bar icon showing a magnifying glass looking at a disk to "Search Directory of Services." On Prodigy, click on the "A-Z" tool at the bottom of the screen, or jump to **boards a-z**. Then search for the name of your hardware or software maker.

You may discover that your hardware or software company has created its own SIG on your consumer service. If so, go there and check it out. A good example: You bought your copy of Datastorm's ProComm Plus for Windows several years ago. Now you've just bought a new 28.8 Kbps Zoom modem. The trouble is, this modem is not on the modem list that came with ProComm Plus.

So you sign on to CompuServe, go to the Datastorm SIG, and download the latest version of a data file called "MODEMS.DAT" that does indeed include information about your new Zoom modem and many other new makes and models. This lets you "install" your new modem for ProComm Plus in a twinkling.

If you come up empty on your company search—and even if you don't—be sure to try a generic search on your Big Three service, using a term like "modem," "ink-jet," "fax software," or whatever.

Though your mileage may vary, in most cases you will find that using the SIGs, clubs, and forums on the Big Three is fast, efficient, and enjoyable because at least one individual is being paid to keep you satisfied. That individual is the system operator or "sysop," a person to whom you can always appeal personally via e-mail.

The Internet Approach

Now let's turn to the Internet. We'll assume that your efforts on one of the Big Three were unfruitful, or that you access the Net via an Internet Service Provider. Where on the Net can you go to find the solution to your problem?

The place to start is with the power searching tools presented in Chapter 17 on page 92. Point your Web browser at **http://www.infoseek.com**, and take advantage of Infoseek's free Web searches. Then go to Yahoo!'s site (**http://www.yahoo.com**). In general, you should search for the name of the company that made your hardware or software so you can find out if the company has a home page.

Ideally, you will discover that the ABC Software Company does indeed have a home page, and that the page contains an area called "Customer Support" or "Frequently Asked Questions" or something else that might hold the answer to your particular problem.

If you want to wing it, you can try to guess at the URL of your target company's home page. For example, if you enter **http://** followed by **www.hp.com**, **www.apple.com**, or **www.microsoft.com**, you will find yourself, respectively, at the home pages for Hewlett-Packard, Apple, or Microsoft.

Tapping Newsgroups

The next step is to check the Internet's collection of newsgroups, which roughly correspond to the SIGs offered on the Big Three services. Even though newsgroups are actually little more than crude player piano rolls of messages, there are a heck of a lot of them and they cover nearly every subject you can imagine.

Newsgroups can be good sources of computer help information. We must tell you, however, that in our tests we found that computer-oriented newsgroups tend to contain a lot more questions than they do answers and thoughtful replies. But that could be a function of the questions we were investigating or even the time of year—like everyone else, computer gurus go on vacation sometime.

In any event, start your newsgroup search by pointing your browser at **http://www.dejanews.com**. DejaNews doesn't cover all available newsgroups, but it does cover the "comp" (computer) hierarchy, and it does let you search through nearly an entire year's worth of postings.

If you find a relevant newsgroup via DejaNews, you might want to add it to your Hotlist, Bookmarks, or your browser's equivalent. That will make it easy to return to the newsgroup in the future. (Don't forget that many Web browsers can also be used to read newsgroups.) You might also consider posting your question to the newsgroup and checking back the next day for answers.

Conclusion

Once again, we cannot claim that the answer to any computer question you might have can be found online. But we can definitely say that your chances of finding answers online are better now than at any time in the past. So although there are no guarantees, you owe it to yourself to check.

Along the way, you might also want to drop in to the Internet Computer Index at **http://ici.proper.com** and the Ziff-Davis home page at **http://www.ziff.com**. Both are interesting, if imperfect, sites that can serve as good starting points for your search for computer help information.

Education

25

Colleges and universities, along with defense contractors and the military, were involved in the Internet from its beginning more than two decades ago. Indeed, it is fair to say that the education community had more to do with developing and shaping the Internet than any other group. So it should come as no surprise that there are a wealth of educational resources, as well as lots of information about specific educational institutions, on the Net and the Web.

In Chapter 8, we looked at the kind of information a major university often provides via the Web. Here, we'll branch out even further to include finding information on elementary and secondary schools (kindergarten through Grade 12), as well as information on college financial aid.

An Elementary Education:
http://hillside.coled.umn.edu

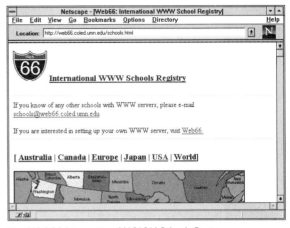

The Web66 International WWW Schools Registry.

Let's start by looking at how to get information on any of several hundred schools—kindergarten through Grade 12—located in the United States, Mexico, and Canada. Cool. But why should you care? Three words: You're being transferred.

If that should happen, you may want to know how to get information about the schools in the state you will soon be calling home. That's why you need to know about the Web66 International WWW Schools Registry. Web66 is a World Wide Web feature made possible by a grant from the 3M Company and put up by the University of Minnesota.

You can start by pointing your browser at **http://hillside.coled.umn.edu**. That's the home page for the Hillside Elementary School in Cottage Grove, Minnesota, and it's the best elementary school site we've seen. It's definitely worth a look, even if your kids are already in junior high.

Moving to Texas

At the bottom of the Hillside Elementary School page, you will see a link for "Some other schools." Click on that, or bypass Hillside completely and point your browser at **http://web66.coled.umn.edu/schools.html**. As you scroll down the resulting Registry, you'll see a map of the entire United States, Mexico, and a good portion of Canada.

Let's assume you're about to move to Fort Worth, Texas. Mouse over to Texas on the map and click. Elementary schools, secondary schools, the Texas Department of Education—the

We clicked on "Texas," and this appeared.

choices go on and on. You know you're going to be in the Fort Worth area, so you click on "Birdville High Schools." The home page for the Birdville Independent School District comes up.

The Birdville Independent School District page.

You scroll down and learn that there are 20 elementary schools, 7 middle schools, and 2 high schools in the Birdville Independent School District (BISD), plus the Shannon Education Center for students with special needs. As you go deeper and deeper, clicking on various hot links, you start to develop a sense of what BISD is all about, the people who make it work, and whether or not you and your kids will be happy there.

Good News/Bad News

We were truly amazed at the number of elementary and secondary schools, and school districts, that have set up home pages on the Web. You should definitely check them out if you're trying to decide where to live when you get transferred.

All is not perfect, however. First, only a fraction of the schools and school districts in a given state are online and accessible from the pages we've suggested here. Second, we have found that you can't always get connected to a given site when you want to. Third, when you do make the connection, there is no telling how good, extensive, or even accurate the information you find will be.

Still, we have no doubt that the overall quality of the elementary and secondary school sites will improve over time. Nor do we hesitate in urging you to check out what is available right now, should a transfer or move be in your future. It's entirely possible that you'll learn something or uncover a contact who can give you information and insights that will help you decide which school district you want to live in.

Colleges and Financial Aid

If there's a college or university you're interested in learning more about, go to Infoseek (**http://www.infoseek.com**) or to some other search engine and do a Web search on the institution's name.

You will also want to check these sites:

- **http://www.petersons.com**
- **http://www.clas.ufl.edu/CLAS/american-universities.html**
- **http://www.mit.edu:8001/people/cdemello/univ.html**

The first site focuses on American universities. The second site has a more international flavor. Neither purports to be comprehensive, but both can be excellent starting points for anyone interested in exploring institutions of higher learning.

Of course, once you've found a college or university of interest, there's the small matter of tuition and other expenses—a matter that often reveals a deep-seated need for financial aid. Certainly you should start with the financial aid programs offered by your college of choice. But often that isn't enough. So what do you do? You check the Web.

The Financial Aid Page

The place to go is Mark Kantrowitz's Financial Aid Information home page. Point your browser at **http://www.cs.cmu.edu/afs/cs/user/mkant/Public/FinAid/finaid.html**. Or, to avoid having to key all that in, simply go to Infoseek and search on "Kantrowitz."

Mr. Kantrowitz is the author of *The Prentice Hall Guide to Scholarships and Fellowships for Math and Science Students*. But his home page covers much more than just math and science. In fact, the hot links in that figure are compacted for your convenience in the initial screen, starting with "What's New?" If you scroll down, you will see the same links presented as a more conventional bulleted list.

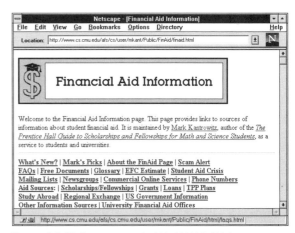

Financial Aid Information on the World Wide Web.

Conclusion: Education Newsgroups

Finally, you won't want to miss the many education-oriented newsgroups. These include the following hierarchies:

- misc.education
- alt.education
- clari.news.education
- k12
- soc.college
- alt.college

Farther down in these hierarchies, you will find groups such as **misc.education.medical**, **misc.education.multimedia**, and **misc.education. science**, as well as **alt.education.alternative**, **alt.education.disabled**, **k12.ed.art**, **k12.ed.music**, and even **alt.college.food** (for discussions of dining halls, cafeterias, mystery meat, food fights, and more).

The evidence is clear: If you have any questions about or interest in education at any level, it is worth your time to check the Internet and the World Wide Web. The coverage is both broad and deep.

Free Software!

Free software, which is to say, shareware, freeware, and public domain software, have long been a vibrant force in the computer field. That's because no huge investment is required. Anyone with access to a computer can create a program. And over the years, tens of thousands of people have done just that.

26

As a result, regardless of the make or model of your computer, you will find scores of word processing, accounting, database, and spreadsheet programs, plus thousands of games, utility programs, music and education programs, investment and tax programs, real estate managers, desktop publishing programs, and typefaces galore.

Indeed, free software programs have been accumulating like autumn leaves. They exist in great piles on floppy disks and CD-ROMs, and in online libraries, making them only a mouse click or two away if you're on the World Wide Web, the Internet, or a Big Three or other commercial system. And, believe it or not, the sheer quantity of free software that is available is a major problem. It's the main obstacle you've got to overcome if this wonderful concept is to fulfill its promise.

An Embarrassment of Riches

The first book we wrote about this field, *How to Get FREE Software!*, was published in 1983. In the years since, we have written many other books and articles about what is now called shareware. We have found that the biggest problem readers and potential users face is *too much choice*!

Whichever software category you select, the number of programs available is simply overwhelming. And who has time to download and test even five educational programs, to say nothing of doing the same for infinitely more complex spreadsheet or database programs?

Finding the Best

Under the circumstances, you might well conclude that you're better off spending money on a commercial program than spending hours downloading and evaluating shareware. And in some cases, you would be absolutely right. For major applications—word processing, communications, spreadsheet, home finance, etc.—you are probably best off going with the leading commercial package in the category.

But that leaves a wide and incredibly diverse range of *other* kinds of software for which you will probably be best off taking the shareware route. For example, children tire of computer games faster than they outgrow shoes, so why not download a bunch of shareware game programs? No need to make sure that they are the very best games in their category. As long as you review them to make sure their content is appropriate, let the little rug rats have at it! The same is true for educational software.

Other kinds of software require a different approach. If you're looking for a software tool that you plan to use on a regular basis, it is worth taking the time to identify the best. And that's where the Web and the entire online world come in.

Go to the appropriate newsgroup, online forum, SIG, or club and simply post a question: "Can anyone recommend a shareware program that will search the files on my disk for key phrases?" "Is there a good program that would let me look at WordPerfect files, even though I don't have that program?" And so on.

People love to share their finds and their opinions with others. So, as long as you've posted to the right location, you will almost certainly get a good response.

Public Domain (PD), Freeware, and Shareware Software

"Public domain" (PD) software is yours to do with as you please, either because it is unsigned or because its author has specifically placed the program in the public domain.

"Freeware" is generally considered to be copyrighted software that is distributed free of charge and without obligation.

"Shareware" is copyrighted, but freely available. In fact, you are encouraged to share it with others. But if you like and regularly use a shareware package, you are duty-bound to send the programmer who created it the small registration fee he or she requests, typically $5 to $25.

In return, you may receive additional documentation, a more powerful version of the program, the opportunity to contact the program's author for help, and free updates or notification of same. Or you may receive nothing more than a clear conscience.

The Association of Shareware Professionals (ASP) is the trade organization in this field. It promotes uniform quality standards among both its programmer and shareware distributor members. For information about the ASP CD-ROM, which contains copies of all ASP member programs, call 800-263-2390. (If you're on CompuServe, key in **go aspcd** to reach the forum that offers all of these programs for download.)

Also, check out the "Shareware Award Winners" list prepared by *PC Magazine* and *MacUser*. (The two sidebars offer samples from these lists.) Or you might want to use a Web search engine to search on a phrase such as "best shareware," "shareware and award," or something similar.

Where to Look for Free Software

The real trick to making the most of shareware is using the online world to smoke out both the names of the best programs and the locations from which they can be downloaded. If no location is given, we advise starting with the libraries on CompuServe or America Online, if you have access to those systems. (To download programs from Prodigy, you've got to join ZD Net, an extra-cost service.)

Using the Big Three

CompuServe has long been a magnet for people who are really into personal computing, so its file collections tend to be deep and broad.

Award-Winning Macintosh Shareware

Each year *MacUser* publishes its "Shareware Awards," including winners and runners-up. This list is an excellent starting point for anyone interested in locating and downloading the best Macintosh shareware.

For a complete copy of the awards list, point your browser at **http://www.zdnet.com**. That will take you to ZD Net (formerly ZiffNet). Click on the *MacUser* icon, and you'll be all set. To download a program of interest on the awards list, you need only click on its name. Or you can use the file names and relevant keywords to search for programs of interest at the Web sites listed in this chapter.

Here are just a few abbreviated examples of some of the winners you will find:

Educational: MPj Astro (MPJASTRO.SIT). "Outstanding astronomy program." View the heavens from any place in the world.

Fun and Games: Realmz (REALMZ.SIT). Tim Phillips and Fantasoft. Role-playing. Crypts, dungeons, castles, and adventure. "It has developed a cult following that many commercial offerings would envy."

Graphics: GraphicConverter (GRACON.SIT). Thorsten Lemke. Translates to or from virtually any graphics format.

Personal Tools: CryptDisk (CRDISK.SIT, demo version). Will Price. Lets you password-protect and encrypt your files. Point your browser at **ftp://ftp.primenet.com/users/w/wprice/README** for more information.

System Enhancements: HoverBar (HOVERB.SIT). Guy Fullerton. Program launcher for System 7.5. Similar to commercial program Square One.

Utilities: StuffIt Expander and DropStuff with Expander Enhancer (STUFEX.SEA and DROPST.SEA). Compress and decompress files using almost any Mac, DOS, or UNIX compression scheme in existence.

In addition, because they are offered by a profit-making enterprise, the files are made available for download only after they've been tested by a sysop to be virus-free and free of any copyright violations. Few, if any, Internet or Web sites make that promise.

If you are a CompuServe subscriber, key in **go macff**, **go pcff**, or **go graphff** to get to the CompuServe "file finder" features you need. You can then search by keyword (up to three keywords can be specified), date, uploader, and so on.

Award-Winning Windows/DOS Shareware

The following greatly abbreviated list of leading shareware programs was extracted from the 1995 Ziff-Davis "Shareware Award Winners and Runners-Up" list that you will find by pointing your browser at **http://www.ziff.com** and selecting either the "shareware awards" hot link at the bottom of the screen or the *PC Magazine* logo from the top of the screen.

When you get to the shareware awards Web site, you will be able to click on the program name itself and download a copy. But you may also want to use the details supplied there as search terms that will help you sharpen your online shareware searching skills.

Here are excerpts from the awards list:

Business and Finance: SEW.ZIP. Scheduling Employees for Windows. Smoothly automates the management of worker time schedules.

Communications: WRAMP.ZIP. WinRamp Lite. Sophisticated, fully featured communications program that can emulate RipScrip, ANSI, TTY, and other popular terminal types.

Major Applications: KH.ZIP. SmartTracker Inventory. Manage data on your personal possessions with organized catalogs accessed from easy-to-use buttons and lists.

Math and Science: TENKEY.ZIP. Replaces the Windows calculator. Provides a 10-key adding machine and a scientific, trigonometric, or financial calculator. Save, print, and reuse tapes; define decimal places; and cut and paste from other applications.

Utilities—DOS: CDQCK.ZIP. CD-Quick Cache. Improves performance of CD-ROM drives. Functions with any CD-ROM extensions or with software that bypasses the extensions. Works with Windows and will not conflict with any hard-disk caches.

Utilities—Windows: TEXTPD.ZIP. Full-featured text editor. Open multiple files. Use toolbar with balloon help to access an extensive variety of useful editing tools including search and replace, block select, file comparisons, and more. Choose fonts, invert cases, print files, and use true drag-and-drop to move text.

America Online has good files, too. We particularly like the long program descriptions AOL permits and the user interface AOL offers to make searching easy. Do a Control-K and specify the keyword **filesearch** to access this feature.

Using the Web

In our opinion, CompuServe and AOL are the places to start, not only because their files are pre-tested for viruses, but also because far fewer people are likely to be trying to use these commercial systems at any given moment than are likely to be using the Internet. That means the searches (and the downloads) tend to be faster than those you will find at Internet sites.

In addition, whether you are using a feature on one of these systems or simply using them to get to the Internet, the connect-time rate is the same. So you've got nothing to lose.

Of course, you will also want to check the Web. Indeed, if you don't use CompuServe or AOL, the Web is likely to be the first place you turn. Here's a starter list of locations we've visited and feel comfortable recommending:

- Global Network Navigator's "Software and Shareware" (Windows, DOS, Macintosh, and other platforms): **http://www.gnn.com/gnn/wic/wics/comput.sof.html**

- Exec-PC's World File Project (Windows, DOS, Macintosh, and other platforms): **http://filepile.com/cgi-bin/start**

- C/net, Inc.'s "Shareware.Com" (Windows, DOS, Macintosh, and other platforms): **http://www.shareware.com**

- Jumbo! "Official Web Shareware Site" (Windows, DOS, Macintosh, and other platforms): **http://www.jumbo.com**

- Virtual Shareware Library (Windows, DOS, and Macintosh): **http://vsl.cnet.com**

- California State University, San Marcos Library Technical Services Windows Shareware Archive (Windows only): **http://www.csusm.edu/cwis/winworld/winworld.html**

- Apple Computer's FTP sites for Apple-related software (Apple/Macintosh only): **http://www.apple.com/documents/sharewaresites.html**

Games

27

FRAN, IF YOU WIN
ONE MORE TIME,
I'M LEAVING YOU.

Lapsed Presbyterians that we are, your co-authors are more than
a little ambivalent about games in general and computer games
in particular. On the one hand, games seem like such an incredible
waste of time—especially when your shelves contain books by
Plato, Shakespeare, Twain, Jane Austen, and Anne Tyler that have
yet to be read.

On the other hand, it was the classic computer game *Adventure* that
was the catalyst for our buying an original IBM PC in the first place,
back in 1981. And *Adventure* is a text-based game with none of the
graphics and sound effects that you find in *Doom* or *Myst*.

Games, Games, and More Games on the Web

The purpose and point of this chapter is to alert you to the fact that
games of every sort are very big on the Web and the Net. Coverage is
not limited to computer games. You will also find programs, information, and fan clubs devoted to classic games like chess, bridge,
backgammon, billiards, and anything else you care to name.

We'll begin by telling a tale about ourselves. Though he doesn't get
much time to play it, Alfred is captivated by *Myst*. So on a recent visit
to Waldenbooks, he paid $20 for a book of *Myst* hints and directions.

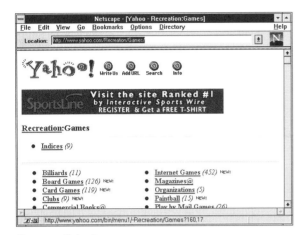

Games on Yahoo!.

Then we began to research this chapter. It quickly became clear that most of the information in the book was available online via the Web. Yes, some effort and knowledge were required to locate it. And admittedly, it is much more convenient to have everything gathered and printed in a book with a good index. But the bottom line is this: If you're paying roughly $3 an hour to access the Internet via one of the Big Three systems, $20 will buy you over six-and-a-half hours of connect time! At a speed of 28.8 Kbps, you could theoretically download the equivalent of that book, including illustrations, for about $1.75.

Our calculations could be off by an order of magnitude, and the difference between the online cost and the cost of the book would still be dramatic. And, of course, *Myst* isn't the only game covered in depth online.

The Leading Game Sites

Hints, tips, and tricks are only one reason for using the Web to pursue an interest in games. You will also find updates and add-ons for your favorite game software. You will find other enthusiasts, all of whom are eager to discuss this hobby, and some of whom may be interested in challenging you to a contest either online or by mail.

If you are interested in a specific game, your best bet is to start with Infoseek, Yahoo!, or one of the other Web search engines. For example, if you were to go to the Infoseek home page at **http://www.infoseek.com** and do a search on "Myst hints," you would encounter, among other things, the following sites:

- Myst FAQ
- The Myst Hints Web Page
- Help for Myst Island
- Ask Dr. Myst

- Where is the Myst book?
- The Hint Web Pages
- The Amended Myst Walkthrough

And these are just a few of the *Myst* sites we found with Infoseek. The search actually turned up more than 100!

Games on Yahoo!: *http://www.yahoo.com/Recreation/Games*

If games of any sort are of interest, you should point your browser at the Yahoo! URL in the subhead above. Once there, click on "Indices," and you'll be taken to a menu that contains links to other master gaming pages, like Pacific HiTech's Game Page of the Universe.

There are also links to topics like billiards, gambling, and paintball. If you scroll down, you will even find links to newsgroups like **rec.games.design** and **rec.games.misc**.

The Game Page of the Universe:
http://www.pht.com/game/universe/index.html

If you're really interested in computer games, you can't afford to miss the Game Page of the Universe, a site sponsored by Pacific HiTech. As the welcoming text says, they are "striving to create and maintain the hottest list of game links from all over the Internet, so if you know of a really cool games site that's not here, please send mail to **peter@pht.com** and if it checks out, he'll add it to this list!"

Here are just a few of the hot links you'll find:

The Game Page of the Universe.

- The Newest in Games from the Internet!—An FTP site directory of computer game files available for downloading.
- The Best of Internet Arcade Games (for DOS)—"Our entire DOS games directory of our FTP site with one-line descriptions for each and every game we have."

- The Best of Internet Arcade Games (for Windows)—PHT's entire Windows games directory of its FTP site with a one-line description for every game.

- The *Doom* Upgrade Home Page—"What? You don't have the newest version of *Doom*? If you don't have v1.9, then you need to visit our *Doom* upgrade home page!"

- Games of All Kinds—"A large collection of games for MS-DOS, MS-Windows, Macintosh, and Linux. Feel free to upload more!"

The site includes links to "Other Cool Game" sites, including Apogee and 3-D Realms, plus links to the Electronic Arts Home Page and the Capstone Software Home Page.

There's also a link to the Games Domain, which bills itself as "the largest list of game companies and gaming information on the Internet." Unfortunately, your co-authors have found access to the U.K.-based Games Domain to be quite slow on numerous visits, but it is still worth a try.

The DoomGate Home Page: *http://doomgate.cs.buffalo.edu*

Finally, what would a chapter about computer games on the Internet be without *Doom* and at least one *Doom* home page? *Doom* is probably the ultimate hand-eye coordination computer game, for the devil knows, there's no plot or story. It is pure shoot-'em-up (or chainsaw-'em-up). Naturally, it is wildly popular.

So, if you're into *Doom*, you can't afford to miss the unofficial Doom-Gate page. Just point your browser at the URL in the subhead above.

Happy gaming, everyone. Heh, heh, heh!

Welcome to DoomGate: Lock and load!

Government and Politics

28

Government affects everyone. And wherever you have government, politics can't be far behind. Interestingly, a great deal of what both government and politics offer us is information, a fact that makes them perfectly suited to the World Wide Web. It's a win-win situation.

For example, a governmental agency can use the Web to fulfill its duty to distribute information and answer questions asked by the citizenry. And we citizens get the answers we need much faster than ever before. It's just possible that the Web will make the phrase "unresponsive bureaucrat" a thing of the past.

As for politics, well, politicians go where the people are, and today that means going online. Politicians benefit by being able to present their messages in more detail than is possible with a ten-second sound bite. Voters benefit by being better informed and by having the ability to easily track what a politician says.

In this chapter, we've chosen six sites relevant to government or politics at the federal level. You will also want to use the search engines discussed in Chapter 17 on page 92 to look for city, state, and local government online resources, as well as to search for the names of politicians, political parties, and the like.

We selected the U.S. Postal Service, the Social Security Administration, the Internal Revenue Service, the Thomas Legislative Information site, and the White House. The place to start, however, is with the Federal Web Locator, a page prepared by Kenneth P. Mortensen and operated by the Villanova Center for Information Law and Policy.

The Federal Web Locator: *http://www.law.vill.edu*

So point your browser at the address shown in the subhead above and select "The Federal Web Locator." The page begins with a list of the latest additions, followed by "Federal Quick Jumps" (hot links to popular federal sites.)

The Federal Web Locator.

That's followed by an extensive list of "Federal Government Web Servers," starting with the legislative, judicial, and executive branches and continuing with "Federal Independent Establishments and Government Corporations" (Central Intelligence Agency, Environmental Protection Agency, Federal Reserve, National Science Foundation, etc.).

Other main categories of sites follow, and the page concludes with "Non-Governmental Federally Related Sites" (*Commerce Business Daily, Congressional Quarterly, Legi-Slate*, etc.)

In the near future, the Federal Web Locator will include searching capabilities, more sites, and other features. This is a super Web site—one not to be missed. (You will also want to check out the Clinton Administration's Business Advisor site at **http://www.business.gov**.)

Zip Codes and More: *http://www.usps.gov*

The Postal Service is the one governmental entity that touches most people most often. Sure, it's the target of criticism and jokes, but what it accomplishes day in and day out is nothing short of remarkable.

Still, we try to avoid actually going to the post office because the lines can be long and they may or may not have the chart or form we need. Far better to point your Web browser at the address shown above.

You'll want to check out all the areas, but start by clicking on "Your Post Office." Among other things, it will take you to a spot where you can look up nine-digit zip codes. Just key in the street or other delivery address, the city, and the state, and the system will tell you which "ZIP+4" zip code to use.

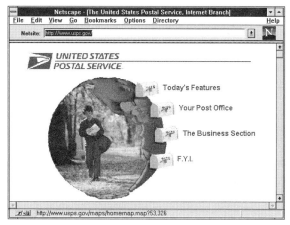

Your post office—open 24 hours a day!

When you think about the time and effort required to thumb through the Postal Service's fat zip code directory, this is a wonderful convenience.

Social Security Online: *http://www.ssa.gov*

The Social Security Administration's Web site offers lots of good information. You might start by scrolling through the home page until you get to "Retirement, Survivors, Disability, and SSI Program Information." Beneath this heading, look for a reference to ANYPIA.EXE, a Windows/DOS program you can download to compute your own retirement benefits.

Elsewhere on the home page you'll find an icon for the "Forms" feature. Click on this and you'll be given the opportunity to download copies of the most requested Social Security forms.

In particular, you may want to get the form called "Request for Earnings and Benefit Estimate Statement (SSA-7004)." This is the form experts advise sending in every few years to make sure that all your Social Security tax payments have been properly recorded. (Forms are available in PDF and PostScript formats. See the "PDF and the Adobe Acrobat Reader" sidebar for more information.)

Instant Tax Forms from the IRS: *http://www.ustreas.gov/treasury/bureaus/irs/taxforms.html*

Have you ever sat down to do your taxes, only to discover along about midnight that you don't have one of the forms you need? And to make matters worse, that form is not among the ones you can normally pick up at your post office, state liquor store, or other location.

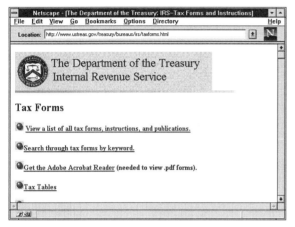

IRS tax forms on the World Wide Web.

Thanks to the U.S. Treasury Department's IRS Web site, you never need face this problem again. Just point your browser at the URL above. From there, you'll be able to view tax tables, browse documents, search through tax forms by keyword, and view a list of all the tax forms, instructions, and publications you can download. (See the "PDF and the Adobe Acrobat Reader" sidebar for information on both the PDF file format referred to on this site and the Adobe Acrobat Reader, which reads PDF files.)

The Congress: *http://thomas.loc.gov*

You'll also want to visit the Thomas Legislative Information site on the Web. This site is hosted by the Library of Congress and got its name from the fact that Thomas Jefferson founded that institution by donating his substantial collection of books to it.

This is the place to go for the full text of legislation, the *Congressional Record*, bill summaries and status, and much more. Both the House and the Senate have hot links here, as does C-SPAN (Cable-Satellite

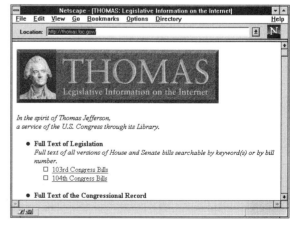

The Thomas Legislative Information site.

PDF and the Adobe Acrobat Reader

The forms offered online by the Social Security Administration and the IRS are available in several different desktop-publishing-style formats. Perhaps the most convenient is the PCL format. You can simply print such a file on any printer that supports Hewlett-Packard's Printer Control Language.

However, we think you'll be happiest with PDF (Portable Document Format) files and a free copy of the Adobe Acrobat Reader. Acrobat and PDF were specifically designed by Adobe Systems to make it easy to exchange documents among many different systems (DOS, Windows, Macintosh, UNIX, etc.), especially over the Internet.

This has always been possible—as long as the files were plain ASCII text. The Acrobat difference is that all the fonts, special characters, shading, and other "document" features are preserved. As a result, the printouts of the PDF versions of IRS and Social Security forms are identical to what you'd get from the government, except you probably use a better quality of paper.

Adobe Systems gives its reader program away for free and makes money selling the software that's used to create PDF files in the first place. You can probably find the reader program in the free software libraries discussed in Chapter 26 on page 145. But it might be easier to just go to the IRS site featured in this chapter and click on "Get the Adobe Acrobat Reader." This is one piece of software no Internet user should be without.

Public Affairs Network). So, too, does the Library of Congress, which has a link to its main page, the place to go if you want to search for a book on a particular topic or by a particular author.

Hail to the Chief!:
http://www.whitehouse.gov

The White House home page is our last stop in this chapter. It's a very attractive page. You'll find press releases, transcripts of daily press briefings, presidential speeches, and lots more.

Not surprisingly, this is also a very political page. You'll find among the images presented here the photo of Bill Clinton as a teenager shaking hands with President

Welcome to the White House!

Kennedy. And, of course, you're not likely to find any speeches or other material that might be politically embarrassing to the White House.

Still, the White House home page offers valuable information, and it's an excellent model for any Webmeister to learn from. If you're a real political junkie, you will also want to visit All Politics at **http://allpolitics.com**, Election Line at **http://www.electionline.com**, and Politics USA at **http://PoliticsUSA.com**. (For some reason, the people who created All Politics and Politics USA chose not to use "www" in their addresses.)

Conclusion

We've covered the legislative and executive branches of government, but for reasons of space, we haven't said anything about the judicial branch. You should know, however, that the Supreme Court has long had a significant presence on the Net. Here are three URLs to check for Supreme Court decisions and other documents:

- **http://www.law.cornell.edu/supct**
- **gopher://info.umd.edu**
  Select "Academic Resources by Topic," then "United States and World Politics," then "United States," and finally, "Supreme Court Documents."

- **ftp://cwru.edu**
  Path: **/hermes/***

Home and Garden

29

Perhaps we should have called this chapter "the Internet where you live," for that's exactly the kind of site you'll find here. And we've got another real-life example of how the Net has been helpful around our little patch of ground.

In Chapter 19 we told you about searching DejaNews (newsgroups) for information on dealing with a woodpecker that was knocking the heck out of the side of the house. Well, we've also had problems with a murder of crows. (Yup, "a murder of crows" is the right term, as is "a pride of lions" or "an exultation of larks." You could look it up.) Hundreds of them descend on our yard and trees and make the most awful racket at about five o'clock many summer mornings.

So we went to the Net and within minutes we discovered that the solution is to play a "scare tape," a tape that endlessly repeats crow and blackbird distress calls. You can get such a tape from your county agricultural extension agent. The tape sounds awful, but it does the trick!

We might never have discovered this solution had it not been for the Internet. It's made a real difference in our home and garden!

Books That Work: *http://www.btw.com*

If you've got a specific problem or question (like rogue woodpeckers or a murder of crows), start with DejaNews or one of the other Internet search engines. That's often the best way to quickly locate the information you need.

But if you are in more of a "magazine frame of mind," go to the Books That Work site. Books That Work (BTW) is a company dedicated to developing "compelling and easy-to-use interactive software for home consumers." Naturally, they hope you'll want to buy some of their products. And, after getting a sense of what they're all about by visiting their site, you just might.

When you go to the BTW home page, you'll see a list of new articles, like "How Much Kitchen Counter Space?" and "Plant of the Month: Sweet Autumn Clematis." But you'll also see that the site has three main areas: "Gardening and Landscaping," "Home Improvement," and "Automotive and Real Estate."

Naturally, all three sections have icons you can click on to get more information about BTW products relevant to a topic. But each section also includes a generous selection of really good articles, tips, and lists of links to other topic-relevant Web sites.

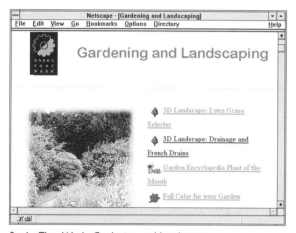

Books That Work: Gardening and Landscaping.

We went to one such site and were presented with information on "Guidelines for Correct Pruning" of trees, complete with high-quality diagrams and other extras that made the Web page look like a page from a textbook. The Books That Work site has lots of genuinely useful information, presented in a very pleasing way. No homeowner should miss it.

This Old House Online: *http://pathfinder.com*

Your co-authors live and work in an eighteenth-century house with a barn for a garage, and a guest cottage we rent out on weekends. In all, we've got three frame structures to maintain. So, yes, you could say

we've been more than a little interested in the PBS television show *This
Old House* over the years. If you like
this kind of thing, too, then you
should definitely visit the *This Old
House* Web site.

Go to the Pathfinder site noted in
the subhead above, then scroll down
that page until you encounter "This
Old House" in highlighted text. Click
on that, and once you arrive at the
site, add it to your Bookmarks or
Favorite Places list. Pathfinder, it

This Old House *online.*

would appear, has deliberately made the URL addresses for the publications it carries so complex that most people are forced to start with
its main home page. (If you want to attempt to go to *This Old House*
directly, the URL is **http://pathfinder.com/@@iAOrMEJYwlAQCZT/TOH**,
so you see what we mean.)

You can use the *This Old House* Web site to learn about the show,
its personalities, and what's coming next. The Web site is part of a triad
that includes the TV show and the magazine of the same name. The
three work together. The show, of course, develops information, tips
and tricks, and other material, which then goes into both the magazine
and the Web page. And the Web page helps generate subscriptions to
the magazine and encourages viewership for the TV show.

The synergy is truly remarkable. It's the kind of thing you'd expect
from Martha Stewart and *Time* magazine, not PBS. Yet here it is.
And the information content is super: "How to Install a Lockset,"
"Using a Circular Saw," "The Right Screw for the Job," and "Saving
Old Windows."

If you like the PBS TV show, you'll like this site, for it maintains the
emphasis on renovating older homes, as opposed to, say, adding a deck
to your late-model "executive home" situated in a former cornfield. Still,
you don't have to own an old house to benefit from the site, since there
are lots of articles about using tools and about any kind of home-
related procedure or technique.

Food, Glorious Food: *http://www.epicurious.com*

If you grew up, as we did, with piles of unopened, unread copies of *Gourmet* magazine in the house, you might well associate the word "stuffy" with that publication.

Maybe it was. Maybe it still is. But one thing we know: Its Epicurious Web site is infused with life, good humor, and a realization that these days no one has time to spend four hours preparing a meal that will be devoured in ten minutes while watching Peter Jennings on the evening news.

Epicurious: For people who eat.

We have no idea what person or company created this site. All we can say is that Condé Nast, the publisher of both *Gourmet* and *Bon Appétit* magazines, has lucked into a real gem of a Webmaster. If you have any interest in food (and drink) at all, you will *love* this site. And by "food," we mean food that real people could really be expected to cook, even after a hard day at work and a long commute. "Recipes," "Forums," "Feedback," "Playing with Your Food," and more—the Epicurious site will tickle your taste buds.

The only caveat is that the Epicurious home page favors large, magazine-page-style graphics and pictures, so it can take a while to load. The other pages are more text-based, and thus, much faster to appear.

Consumer Information Center, Pueblo, Colorado: *http://www.gsa.gov/staff/pa/cic/cic.htm*

Finally, have you ever encountered a TV or radio ad that focused on free or low-cost information from the federal government? Does the address "Pueblo, Colorado" have a familiar ring? If so, and even if this is all passing strange, you should know about the federal government's Consumer Information Center (CIC).

The government, which is to say, our taxes, support a mini-information industry designed to research topics of interest and then write and produce booklets summarizing the findings. Sample titles have included "Movement, Growth, and Mortality of American Lobsters (*homarus americanous*) Tagged Along the Coast of Maine" and "The Hammered Dulcimer in America," a 93-page publication studying "the role of the hammered dulcimer in the musical history of the United States."

The taste of Maine lobsters and the sounds of the hammered dulcimer are two of our favorite things in life. But we weren't aware that we had helped pay for studies of them. Nor were we aware, until we sent a request to Pueblo, Colorado, some years ago, that there is a catalogue of government studies that

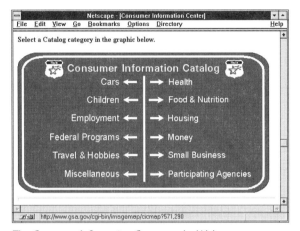

The Consumer Information Center on the Web.

includes booklets on everything from "Helping Your Child Get Ready for School" to "Lesser Known Areas of the National Park System" to the "Motorist's Tire Care and Safety Guide."

Basically, the CIC publishes something for nearly everyone. In years past we have sent for the catalogue, found several items of interest, and sent in a check and an order for several publications. And the publications were not only cheap, they were also quite good.

Now those publications are on the Web. They can be downloaded at no cost, and all you give up are the graphic images, which are usually more for visual relief than for anything else. So we'd all be fools not to take advantage of this service. Cars, children, health, housing, money, employment, food and nutrition, and many more general topics are covered.

There's no need to send for a catalogue and then fill out an order form. Hit the Net, go to the Consumer Information Center Web site, click on a publication name, and it will be quickly sent to your computer, from which you can print it once you are offline.

Humor

30

JUST A MINUTE, SWEETHEART. MOMMIE'S DOWNLOADING FROM "STRESS-NET."

Whenever Alfred calls home, his dad has a really good joke or "story" for him. Much of the time, the jokes are as current as the morning's headlines, so you wonder how in blazes jokes get dispersed so quickly—particularly to people in their 70s who own neither a fax machine nor a personal computer.

All you can surmise is that a telephone and a friend of a friend who heard it from her stockbroker must be in the loop somewhere. Either that, or your parents are secretly on SeniorNet and regularly tap into the great underground electronic joke stream.

In all seriousness, the speed with which a funny story, joke, or *bon mot* travels across the country—or around the globe—is a subject worthy of a doctoral thesis. And that's just using one-to-one telephone connections. With the Web's "one-to-many" communications, the reach is both global and instantaneous.

Decoding ROT-13 Jokes

The newsgroup **rec.humor.funny** is one of the most popular groups on the Net. Point your browser at **news:rec.humor.funny**. (Notice that there are no forward slashes ("//") in URLs for newsgroups.)

This group accepts jokes from everywhere, but only those judged to be truly funny are posted by the moderator, Brad Templeton. Inevitably, some jokes are bound to offend some people. To shield such sensitive souls from encountering something distasteful, some jokes are encoded like this: *"Gurfr ner gur gvzrf gung gel zra'f fbhyf . . ."*

The technique used to encode this and other jokes on the Net is called ROT-13. This simply means that the alphabet is rotated 13 characters so that an "a" appears as an "n," a "b" as an "o," and so on.

The easiest way to decode this kind of text is to capture the encoded joke as a text file and then run a program called ROT13.EXE against it. The file will be displayed on the screen, with all encoded text now readable.

ROT13.EXE is widely available on the Net in versions for every computer. (See the Internet Toolkit and Glossbrenner's Choice Appendix of this book for information on the DOS/Windows version. If you're a Macintosh user, see Chapter 26 for pointers to the places that offer Mac programs online.)

All of which is by way of saying that the quantity of humor you can tap into via the Internet is almost unbelievable. Jokes, cartoons, sound clips, video clips—regardless of format, if someone thinks it's funny, it's probably on the Net somewhere.

Start with Yahoo!:
http//:www.yahoo/com/Entertainment/Humor_Jokes_and_Fun

The place to begin is with Yahoo!. Point your browser at the above address to go directly to the humor collection. Or go to **http://www.yahoo.com** and then select "Entertainment: Humor, Jokes and Fun."

What you'll find is a double-column list containing nearly 50 different categories. These range from "Absurd," "Anagrams," "British Humor," and "Fortune Cookies" to "Lawyer Jokes," "Palindromes," "Practical Jokes," and Usenet newsgroups devoted to humor.

Now, if you are a humor aficionado, it may profit you to use Infoseek or DejaNews to search for specific kinds of jokes using phrases like "cats and humor," "lightbulb and joke," and so on. But we still feel that Yahoo! is the place to start.

The Late Show with David Letterman: http://www.cbs.com:80/lateshow

It's fair to say that there are at least two types of humor resources online: organized and informal. The sites and newsgroups you will go to via Yahoo! are mostly informal, which means that in most cases, anything goes.

The more formal and focused sites are best represented by the home page for *The Late Show with David Letterman*. This is one of several TV-show home pages you can access when you go to **http://www.cbs.com**.

When you get to the *Late Show* home page, you will be greeted by the Top Ten list presented on the most recent edition of the show. You can also get a list of who is scheduled to appear on the show in the coming week. But what you'll probably want to do is click on the icon for the "Late Show Top Ten."

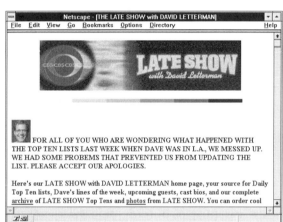

Heeere's Dave!

That will take you to a spot where you can search Dave's Top Ten items on the basis of a keyword. We tried "Hillary Clinton" and were rewarded with nearly 30 Top Ten lists—everything from "Questions Congress Asked Hillary Clinton" to "Ways Clinton Can Improve His Approval Rating" to "White House Christmas Traditions." So what can you say, it's just Dave being Dave. If you're a Letterman fan, you can't afford to miss this site.

The Capitol Steps

If you're a political junkie, you will also want to look at the Capitol Steps site at **http://pfm.het.brown.edu/people/mende/steps**. The Capitol Steps is a comedy troupe made up of former congressional aides. Our assumption is that the group's name has something to do with Mr. and Mrs. John Dean of Watergate fame, but we could be wrong.

In any event, the troupe's stock-in-trade is humorous renditions of familiar songs, some of which you will find at their site. And, the chances are that if you have a Macintosh or multimedia PC, you'll be able to sample aural excerpts of the group's comedy.

Conclusion? Ha!

Humor in its many forms is a vital part of life, so, naturally, you will find tons of it on the Web. There is so much funny stuff online that we could write an entire book about it.

But why bother? With the sites we've pointed you to here, you'll be able to find a good joke on nearly any topic you can imagine. And, most importantly, you'll have fun doing it!

Jobs and Careers

31

If you think the Web might be a good place to look for a job, you're absolutely right. In fact, there is so much material, so many resources, and so many places to look that you could make that your full-time job.

Fortunately, the majority of these resources have been pulled together into a single master menu, which we'll tell you about in this chapter. First, however, let us give you one of the best electronic job-finding tips ever.

Take Full Advantage of Newsgroups

As you may have heard, not all jobs are advertised, and the best jobs almost never are. That's why we advise anyone interested in changing jobs or finding one for the first time to take full advantage of the subject- or industry-relevant Internet newsgroups.

Participating in newsgroups gives you a chance to get to know managers and other employees at companies where you want to work. More importantly, it lets them get to know *you*.

You can't rush things. You've got to build your relationships over time. So it's important to start six months to a year before you expect to land the job. But once you have developed those relationships, it will be perfectly natural to let it be known that you're seriously thinking of making a move. (Obviously, you'd want to do this via a private e-mail message, not by posting to the group.)

The point is that the people you meet this way are already "inside." They are in a position to know about open positions. And now they know you. Certainly there are no guarantees. But ask yourself what you would do in their shoes: Go through the hassle of advertising the job and interviewing complete strangers, or turn to someone they already know?

The Great "Ray and Taylor" Employment Information Site: *http://www.lib.umich.edu/chdocs/employment*

As we explained in Chapter 20, the Clearinghouse for Subject-Oriented Internet Resource Guides is a project of the University of Michigan. Among its guides is one by Philip Ray and Bradley Taylor. It's called "Job Search and Employment Opportunities: Best Bets from the Net."

This regularly updated list of clickable hot links is without a doubt one of the leading "master lists" of job and career information on the Net. Here is what you can expect to find. Each of the "Best Bets" is a clickable link, as are the bulleted items beneath each "Best Bet."

Click on "Best of the Best," for example, and you'll be taken to a page offering links to Academe This Week and the Online Career Center. Click on "Best Bets in Career Development Resources" and you'll find, among other things, links to the complete text of the *Occupational Outlook Handbook* and the *U.S. Industrial Outlook*.

Most important of all, each "Best Bets" page contains an informative description of the resource. This makes it much easier to tell whether a given resource is likely to be of help to you:

- Best of the Best
  - Academe This Week
  - Online Career Center (OCC)
- Best Bets in Education and Academe
  - Academic Physician and Scientist
  - Academic Position Network
  - Jobs at Specific Colleges and Universities
  - University of Minnesota College of Education's Job-Search Bulletin Board
- Best Bets in the Humanities and Social Sciences
  - Job Openings for Economists (JOE)
  - Library and Information Science Placement Service
  - Scholarly Societies Project
- Best Bets in Science and Technology
  - American Institute of Physics
  - American Mathematical Society
  - Bionet
  - Career Mosaic
  - Computing Jobs Newsgroups
  - IEEE-USA Job Listing Service
  - The Monster Board
  - Resume Posting Newsgroup
- Best Bets in Business and Government
  - FedWorld
  - Medsearch America
  - Yahoo!: Employment
- Best Bets in Career Development Resources
  - Career Assistance from the Online Career Center
  - Catapult
  - *Occupational Outlook Handbook* and *U.S. Industrial Outlook*
- Appendixes
  - Best Bets for Extending Your Search: Other Internet Job Guides
  - Best Bets for Navigating the Internet: Tips for Beginners

The Online Career Center: *http://www.occ.com*

If you're serious about looking for job information on the Internet, you'll want to spend some time exploring the Online Career Center (OCC). This site lets you search for job postings by industry, by state, or by city. But you can also search by keyword—that's probably the best way to get your feet wet and to get a sense of what OCC is all about.

You'll also want to check the "Career Assistance" area for advice from Joyce Lain Kennedy, the widely syndicated career columnist, and others. And you may want to explore the resume section. You can indeed put your own resume on OCC. You can even do so in HTML format with colors, pictures, and hot links, but your time may be better spent on your job hunt than in laboring over an HTML resume that busy professionals may not want to take the time to look at!

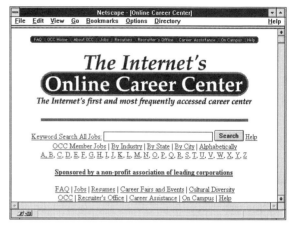

The Internet's Online Career Center.

Medicine

32

In our area, the owner of a discount clothing store used to say in his TV commercials, "An educated consumer is our best customer." Well, if you think about yourself not as a patient but as a consumer of medical services, you can become quite well-educated on the Web.

Someone you know may be ill, and you want to find out more about the disease or condition. Or, your personal doctor may have recommended a certain course of treatment, but you want to know more about your options before going forward. You want what amounts to a second opinion.

Of course, we're not suggesting that you try to diagnose a problem or treat it yourself based solely on what you find on the Internet. When it comes to medical matters, a little knowledge can be a dangerous thing. But if you think about using the Web and the Net to become an informed consumer, you won't go far wrong.

The Virtual Hospital: *http://vh.radiology.uiowa.edu*

You may want to start by taking a moment to look at Yahoo!'s list of medical resources (**http://www.yahoo.com/Health/Medicine**), if only to get a sense of the vast amount of information that's available. You'll find nearly 60 main topics ranging from acupuncture to epidemiology to journals to otolaryngology (nose, ear, and throat specialty) to veterinary science. When you click on a topic, you may find as many as 90 or more relevant items.

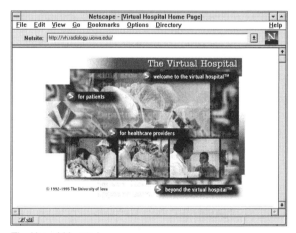

There's nothing wrong with that, of course. It's just that, as is the case with all Web search engines, the results of such ad hoc lists can be such a jumble. The Virtual Hospital, in contrast, has the kind of internal continuity and organization that is possible only when someone or some group sits down to design and create a site.

The Virtual Hospital.

When you go to the Virtual Hospital, click on the "Welcome" selection to read a single page introducing you to the site. Then move on to the "For Patients" feature and take a look at the "Iowa Health Book."

Under the topic "Healthy Living," for example, you'll find a page called "Information About Your Heart." Since a very good friend of ours recently had bypass surgery, we clicked on that. It brought us to a page offering links to information on heart-healthy cookbooks, cardiac rehabilitation calisthenics, cardiac catheterization guide, and much more. We clicked on the cookbooks link and were presented with a list of over a dozen titles, including *The Living Heart Diet* and *Pass the Pepper, Please!: Healthy Meal Planning for People on Salt-Restricted Diets.*

We returned to the "Iowa Health Book" page and clicked on "Total Hip Replacement." We were rewarded with an eight-page, nicely illustrated guide prepared by the Department of Orthopedic Surgery and others at the University of Iowa.

Beyond the Virtual Hospital

The Virtual Hospital includes a search feature, which you can access from the main home page or via the URL **http://vh.radiology.uiowa.edu/Misc/Search.html**. You should definitely try this, but, for best results, be sure to take the time to read the instructions for entering search terms.

You should also be sure to click on "Beyond the Virtual Hospital" on the main page. You'll be taken to a page titled "Other Internet Health Science Resources" that is truly amazing. The contents include "General Resources," "Radiology Departments," "Cancer Resources," "Dermatology Resources," "Women's Health Resources," and more. The actual clickable links occupy some four-and-a-half printed pages. There's so much here, in fact, that your best bet is to print the file with your browser program and then review the list offline. That way you won't miss anything, and you'll know right where to go when you return to this part of the Virtual Hospital.

Certainly, no site can include every aspect of a given field. There are undoubtedly medical subjects that are not covered by the Virtual Hospital. If that's the case, you can turn to Yahoo!, Infoseek, and other search engines. But start with the Virtual Hospital—you really will appreciate its quality and sense of organization.

Movies and Television

33

"DARLING, LIKE THE WEB, I CAN'T DOWNLOAD YOU FAST ENOUGH."

Okay. We've covered art, books, education, government, medicine, and similar topics. Now we move on to what's really important: movies and television! After all, how do most of us spend large portions of our leisure time? We watch TV and we watch movies, whether on the big screen or via videocassette. So you can bet this is a huge area on the Web, and we've got some really neat sites to tell you about.

The Movie Review Query Engine:
http://www.cinema.pgh.pa.us/movie/reviews

The Movie Review Query Engine is a creation of the Pittsburgh Cinema Project, and it gets an automatic point from us for using the term "movie" instead of "film." Real people go to movies. Only professional critics attend screenings of films.

This site is anything but glamorous, at least on the surface. But it's Friday night, you're up for a flick, but you've been too busy to read any reviews. So which movie do you choose?

Get out the newspaper and turn to the entertainment section to find out what's playing. Then sign on to the Movie Review Query Engine and run a search on the name of the movie. We did exactly that for the movie *Get Shorty*. The Movie Review Query Engine came back with a list of about a dozen reviews, each of which included either the reviewer's name or the name of the publication where the review appeared.

Reviews from *Time*, *People*, and *Entertainment Weekly* were on the list. It's like calling up an instant magazine page. Truly cool. But that's only for starters. We'll leave you to discover the other features (such as "Box Office Grosses" and "Movie Bulletin Boards") on your own. Clearly, though, this is one site you do not want to miss.

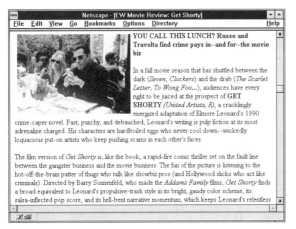
Movie reviews on the Net.

The Internet Movie Database: *http://rte66.com/Movies*

Have you ever wondered after watching a movie, "By golly, who was the actor who played so-and-so?" or "Has this director ever done any other movies?" If you have, then you will want to know about the Internet Movie Database. It includes biographies and filmographies on hundreds of thousands of actors, actresses, and directors; movie trivia;

ratings and reviews; and even some sound and picture files. And almost all of this information is *searchable!*

Searchable? Yes. You can search by movie title, cast or crew member, genre, location, soundtrack, and more. For example, since seeing him in *Enchanted April* (1991), we have been fans of the actor Alfred Molina. You simply would not believe that this is the same actor who starred in the 1995 movie *The Perez Family*. But the Internet Movie Database reveals all, including the fact that Mr. Molina was also in *Raiders of the Lost Ark*, *Ladyhawke*, and *Maverick*, and that he was born in London on May 24, 1953. (He's *British*, for heaven's sake! You could have knocked us over with a feather.)

The Ultimate TV List:
http://www.tvnet.com/UTVL/utvl.html

Above are our picks for movie-related sites ("Two thumbs up" from Alfred and Emily!). Now let's move to television, a.k.a. the "plug-in drug."

Well, yes, TV can be seen as a drug of sorts. But so can the Web. And, as far as we're concerned, if the Web and the Net can make our couch potato hours more productive, so much the better.

If you watch television at all, you will want to visit the TV Net site at the URL given in the subhead above. This URL bypasses the TV Net home page, which you will find takes forever to load because of all the graphic images. (If you have time on your hands, you can reach the TV Net home page at **http://tvnet.com/TVnet.html**.)

The key thing to know about the Ultimate TV List site is that it contains nearly 3,000 links (including links to about 690 Web pages) for almost 550 shows. In a word, it's loaded!

Mad About You, for Example

As an erstwhile presidential candidate might say, "Now, here's the thing, see." We like the Ultimate TV List so much because it makes it easy to locate and visit Web sites devoted to your favorite TV shows. It used to be that if you wanted to learn about all the Internet sites with information on, say, *Seinfeld*, you had to download a FAQ file, print it out, identify the sites that were of interest, and then go back online and laboriously key them in.

The Ultimate TV List does away with that. Sign on and click on "TV Net Search." Key in the name of a show (we used *Mad About You*), and bingo-bongo, a page appears that presents links to virtually all of the sites and locations on the Internet devoted to that program. Our reaction: Wow!

Among other things, our search-results page contained links to an episode guide, the **alt.tv.mad-about-you** newsgroup, a FAQ file, and a series of Web pages that included the official NBC-sponsored *Mad About You* page and the Helen Hunt page.

Whether you're into movies or television or both (and who isn't?), you will love the sites presented in this chapter. So check 'em out!

Personal Finance and Investing

34

LOUISE AND FRED RACK UP ANOTHER SALE FROM THEIR "PET EMPOWERMENT CATALOG"

There are far more investment-related sites on the Web than we can tell you about in a single chapter. But you can't go far wrong if you start with the Personal Finance Center and the Clearinghouse guide discussed below. We'll also tell you where to get free stock quotes and copies of documents that public companies must file with the Securities Exchange Commission.

The Personal Finance Center:
http://www-e1c.gnn.com/gnn/meta/finance/pfcabout.html
The Personal Finance Center (PFC) is the creation of O'Reilly & Associates, one of the first and most successful of all Internet book publishers. It is offered as part of the free Global Network Navigator (GNN) site, which is now owned by America Online.

With those credentials, you'd think PFC would be absolutely stunning. But the graphics are three times bigger than they should be and thus take some time to appear, even at 28.8 Kbps. And the text pages are far too long, with navigation buttons to take you back and forth through the site buried at the very bottom of the page.

That said, however, you will find the information offered by PFC to be quite impressive. The Personal Finance Center consists of three primary areas:

- "Editor's Notes"
- "Features"
- "Internet Resources"

"Editor's Notes" and "Features"

"Editor's Notes" is a short weekly column written by Robert Carroll, the editor of PFC. Past topics have included the nanny tax, finding consumer tips on the Net, the Electronic Credit Repair Kit, and do-it-yourself goldmining.

The second main area is "Features." Click on this to be taken to a database of recently published articles, columns, and interviews, as well as an archive of past articles. At this writing, for example, you'll find such online books as *Investment Strategies for the 21st Century* and *The Mortgage Applicant's Bible.* New chapters for each of them appear every two weeks. There's also a column called "Money Matters" and one called "The Internet Investor."

The archive includes a Q&A area with questions from PFC users and expert answers. The archive also contains articles on investing, true stories of investments by PFC users, interviews, a special section containing favorite articles on real estate, and more.

"Internet Resources"

Finally, the "Internet Resources" area offers a collection of links to personal finance resources available on the Internet. The page also contains a link to "NCSA What's New: Investment and Personal Finance," a collection of links to recently announced services.

You can browse by subjects, including investment, credit cards, home finance and real estate, banking, financial planning, and taxes.

Or you can browse by type of resource, including Web resources, newsgroups and FAQs, mailing lists, Gophers, and shareware.

The "Internet Resources" area may be the most useful section that PFC offers. When it offers you a newsgroup of interest—such as **misc.invest.funds**, a group devoted to sharing information about stock, bond, and real estate funds—you can click on the name and you'll be taken to the latest postings. The same is true for the other kinds of resources on the list.

Clearly, despite the lack of sparkle in its design, the GNN Personal Finance Center is an excellent place to start if you're interested in any aspect of personal finance and investing.

From the Clearinghouse: "Personal Finance Resources on the Internet" at *http://www.lib.umich.edu/chouse/inter/28.html*

Your next stop should be the Clearinghouse, that wonderful collection of subject-specific files that lives at the University of Michigan (see Chapter 20.) Point your browser at the URL given above, and you will be taken to a screen from which you can request a plain text file compiled by Abbot Chambers and Catherine Kummer.

The title of this collection is "Personal Finance Resources on the Internet," and its main topics include investment, financial planning, taxes, home ownership, real estate and mortgages, credit and credit cards, insurance, and financial software. The file date when we visited was 1994, but it is still a good place to start.

Best Credit Card Rates

Our local newspaper occasionally publishes a list of banks offering low-rate credit cards, no fee cards, and so forth. But it's never there when we need it. What to do? Check the Net for the latest information, updated and distributed monthly by CardTrak of America, publishers of the *CardTrak* consumer credit card newsletter.

You'll find the list at a site maintained by the Ram Research Group. Go to **http://www. ramresearch.com/choices.html** and click on "CardTrak." Once you've identified a couple of banks whose offers you're interested in, call **800** directory assistance for their toll-free phone numbers.

All the relevant newsgroups are identified and profiled, as are the relevant FAQ files for each topic. But you will also find mailing lists like "The Weekly Futures Market" or "FedTax-L." And there are Telnet features like Martin Wong's "Market Summary and News," which offers same-day stock prices and daily market news updates.

In the software section, you'll be told where to find Windows/DOS and Macintosh programs to do things like write your checks, track mutual funds and other investments, manage your portfolio, and much more.

Stock Quotes

Lots of sites on the Web offer stock quotes at no charge. But these quotes are always delayed by at least 15 minutes. For access to real-time quotes, you will probably be charged about $50 a month.

Similarly, all of the Big Three online services offer delayed stock quotes and other information, often at no extra charge beyond what you pay to access the Internet through them. And you may be able to download quotes in a format that your investment portfolio management software can import and manipulate.

MIT's Experimental Stock Market Data:
http://www.ai.mit.edu/stocks.html

One of the neatest places to get stock quotes and graphs is from the MIT Artificial Intelligence Laboratory. Created by Mark C. Torrance, this site provides recent stock market information, including the previous day's closing prices, one-year historical graphs of prices, general market news, and quotes for selected stocks. It's updated automatically, usually between 7 and 9 P.M. Eastern Standard Time.

For an example of the kinds of graphs and charts this site produces, we looked at a chart of

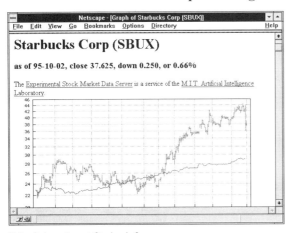

What's brewing at Starbucks?

Starbucks's stock. When you visit this site, be sure to click on "Other finance information available on the Web."

Security APL's Quote Server: *http://pawws.secapl.com*

A company called Security APL has established a site it calls "PAWWS" (Portfolio Accounting World Wide from Security APL). This site is designed to let you handle every aspect of your investment planning by yourself—everything from research to entering trading orders.

For example, you can enter your existing investment portfolio into the PAWWS accounting system, then call up reports and graphs that tell you how its value is changing either in real time or with a 15-minute delay.

PAWWS offers hyperlinks to investment research services. Its "Hotlist" lets you track your hot stocks. There's an "Investment Alert" and a "Stock Alert" service, as well as a brokerage service for making your trades.

Quotes delayed 15 minutes are available free to everyone. Real-time quotes are available only if you open a brokerage account through PAWWS. Brokerage services are provided by Howe Barnes Investments.

EDGAR at NYU

All publicly held companies—which is to say, all companies that sell stock to the public—are required by the U.S. government's Securities Exchange Commission (SEC) to file detailed financial forms at regular intervals. For the past 20 years or so, the only way to gain access to this information online was to subscribe to a service called "Disclosure, Inc."

Now, at long last and after many delays, EDGAR (Electronic Data Gathering and Retrieval Project) is online and set up to provide electronic access to 10K, 8Q, and other iterations of these forms. Just point your browser at **http://edgar.stern.nyu.edu** to reach EDGAR at New York University's Stern School of Business. This is not the most graphical of sites, but it has been built with enthusiasm, and it also offers a lot of valuable non-SEC information.

Science

35

*One of the main goals of this book is to get you to "think Web."
The answer to life and the secrets of the universe could be only
a few keystrokes away—but that won't matter if you haven't
developed the habit of turning to your computer when you have
a question.*

We've got the perfect real-life example. In November 1995, the Hubble
Space Telescope sent back some of the most breathtaking color images
humankind has ever seen. Technically, the images were of the "gaseous
pillars in M16, the Eagle Nebula." In reality, they were images of stalag-
mites of star matter some 4 trillion miles long—the birthing chamber
of stars.

After the Hubble images appeared on TV, the next day's paper printed them in black and white. We read the story, looked at the photo, and simultaneously said, "Let's check the Web!"

Within three minutes, we had a full-color image of the Hubble photo on the screen. It took longer to print than it did to find it. Now *that*, we submit, is the future. That kind of instant access to images, information, and, eventually, sound is where the World Wide Web and the Internet are headed.

But, you've got to remember to look! You've got to develop the Web reflex: "I want X, and I'll bet I can find it on the Web." We've given you the tools to find what you want (check Chapters 17 through 20 again if you need a refresher). The next step is for you to develop the habit and the mindset.

Incidentally, if you want to retrieve the Hubble images yourself, point your browser at **http://www.stsci.edu/pubinfo/PR/95/44.html**. That's the NASA page where we found them. To reach the NASA home page, go to **http://www.nasa.gov**. If you're interested in anything having to do with stars or the planets, you cannot afford to miss this site.

The Clearinghouse for Science:
http://www.lib.umich.edu/chouse/tree/sci.html

If your interests are more down-to-earth—and concern science in general—then the place to start is with the Clearinghouse at the University of Michigan.

Point your browser at the address given above. There you'll find a list containing scores of clickable links dealing with science. The list starts with "Agriculture" and continues on to "Aquatic Biology," "Climate Research," "Energy," "Physics," and more. Each link on *this* page takes you to *another* Clearinghouse page that presents you with a series of selected links aimed at the best Internet locations or Web sites known at the time about that topic.

In our opinion, you'll do best by starting with the Clearinghouse. Then, if you can't find what you need, go to Infoseek, Alta Vista, Yahoo!, or some other search engine.

The Electronic Zoo: *http://netvet.wustl.edu/e-zoo.htm*

The Electronic Zoo lives at Washington University in St. Louis and is directed by veterinarian Ken Boschert. Its purpose is to make it easy to locate any Internet resource dealing with animals, including not only Web sites, but also mailing lists, Telnet locations, FTP sites, Gophers, newsgroups, and more.

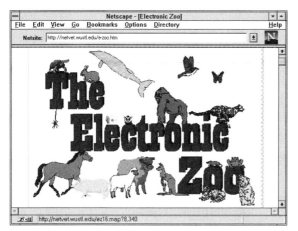

The Electronic Zoo.

On the site's main page, we clicked on the icon for "Animals" and were taken to a page that included icons for "Amphibians," "Birds," "Cows," "Reptiles," and more. There's even an icon labeled "Fictional" consisting of an image of "Bill the Cat" from the Bloom County comic strip.

We clicked on the real "Cats" icon and were taken to a page with the categories "Pet Cats," "Big Cats," "Other," and "Commercial." Under each heading were dozens of clickable links, including, of course, "Socks, the White House Cat." Newsgroups like **alt.animals.felines.snowleopards** were also included, as were links to commercial sites like "Cat Treat of the

Ask Dr. Science: *news:k12.ed.science*

The newsgroup **k12.ed.science** has become a truly cool location for kids with questions about science. There's no formal feature called "Ask Dr. Science," but the scientists, professors, and teachers who frequent this group have made a special point of answering science-oriented questions posted by kids.

Prepare your question offline. Then use the **news:** URL given above. If you're using Netscape, click on the Post icon. Key in a sentence like, "Here's my question:" and then click on Attachment to attach the file you prepared offline. Check back in a day or so to see if you have gotten any answers.

Questions we've seen in this group include, "Why does ice expand?," "What causes cyclones?," and "Can you tell me about mammoth ivory?"

Month Club," "The IAMS Company," and a site called "Finding Your Inner Purr."

Similar resource pages are available for nearly any kind of animal you can name. And we haven't even talked about veterinary medicine and the more scholarly side of things. The Electronic Zoo is a wonderful Web resource, one that neither you nor your kids will want to miss.

The Smithsonian: *http://www.si.edu/start.htm*

The Smithsonian Institution calls itself "America's Treasure House for Learning." So it could fit quite comfortably into any number of subject-specific chapters. We've chosen to put it under "Science" because we wanted to talk about airplanes. Specifically, we wanted to find out about the Wright Brothers.

So we went to the URL given above and clicked on "search" in the very first paragraph of welcoming information. That gave us the opportunity to search the Smithsonian Web, the National Museum of Natural History, the National Museum of American Art, or the National Air and Space Museum. (You know which one we picked!)

A search on "Wright Brothers" turned up about 20 clickable links, ranked in order of relevance to the

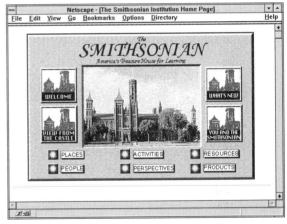

Welcome to the Smithsonian.

search term. The first three items were digitized images. The seventh item was "Pioneers of Flight," which led to a page offering images and text, starting with the Wright EX biplane and ending with the human-powered Gossamer Condor.

The Smithsonian is and always will be a very special place. Its Web site is no exception. It will inform and delight you and yours for hours.

Sports

36

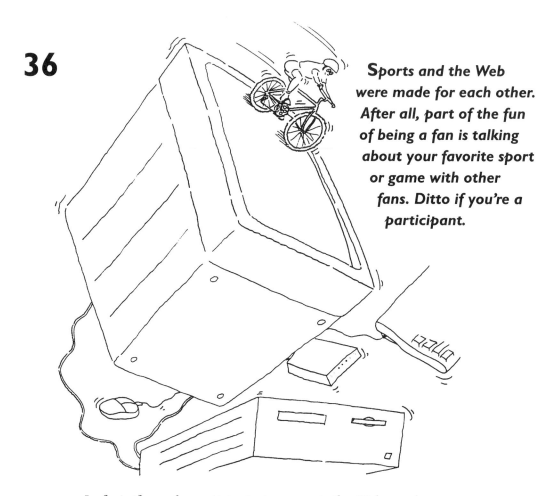

Sports and the Web were made for each other. After all, part of the fun of being a fan is talking about your favorite sport or game with other fans. Ditto if you're a participant.

In fact, if you do participate in a sport, the Web can be even more useful to you. Scuba divers can exchange tips on the best dive sites in various parts of the world. If you're a squash player, you can get advice on that new racket you're thinking about buying. Paintball players can discuss strategies and arrange future contests.

What's the Score?:
http://www.usatoday.com/sports/sfront.htm
You get the picture: Regardless of your sport of interest, regardless of whether you're a participant or a fan, the Web and the Net have a lot to offer. Starting, of course, with sports scores.

Go to the URL above to reach the *USA Today* sports home page. When you click on the "Scores" button in the lower right corner, you'll be taken to a page offering the day's scores. If you plan to visit often, take a moment to add the scores page to your list of Bookmarks, Favorite Places, or whatever your browser program calls the feature that lets you record URLs.

The *USA Today* scores pages cover basketball, baseball, college

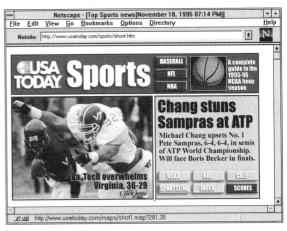

USA Today sports.

football, hockey, and more. The information for each contest is continually updated: You'll be told when the game begins, the score at each quarter or period, and the final score when the game is over. If you click on, say, "Michigan vs. Penn State," you'll be taken to a page that gives you more detail, such as the number of first downs, number of yards rushing, individual player statistics, and so forth.

As you would imagine, the *USA Today* site has a lot of additional sports information and features. But we'll let you discover them for yourself. The main thing is that this is a very good place to start.

Three Great Sports Sites and Sports Newsgroups

You'll also want to check out the sites operated by *Sports Illustrated*, ESPNET, and the *Raleigh News & Observer*. Here's where to point your browser:

- *Sports Illustrated*: **http://pathfinder.com**
- ESPNET Sports Zone: **http://ESPNET.Sports.Zone.com**
- *Raleigh News & Observer* Sports Server: **http://www2.nando.net/SportServer**

The first time you visit the *Sports Illustrated* site, you pretty much have to start with the Pathfinder magazine feature, with its elaborate graphics that take forever to load. But once you are there, simply add it to your Bookmarks or Favorite Places list so that in the future you can skip Pathfinder and go directly to the *Sports Illustrated* site.

All three locations offer features, interviews, photos, and columns. But the Sports Server is particularly good at offering you links to other sports resources and sites on the Web. You can even use a feature called "Score" to create a custom page for the sports and teams you're interested in.

Also, don't miss the many sports-related newsgroups on the Net. See Chapter 19 or Glossbrenner's Choice in the appendix for information on getting the complete list of newsgroups. In the meantime, check out the rec.sport hierarchy. Point your browser at one of these locations:

- **news:rec.sport.baseball**
- **news:rec.sport.basketball.women**
- **news:rec.sport.hockey.field**
- **news:rec.sport.football.college**
- **news:rec.sport.soccer**

The Award-Winning GolfWeb:
http://www.golfweb.com

Though both of your co-authors have Scottish ancestors, neither of us plays golf or knows anything about the fine art of knocking a little white ball around an artificially created "natural" space. Of course, golfers might say the same about our passion for fly fishing, a sport in which actually catching a fish isn't really the point.

So why are we featuring the GolfWeb site here? Because it is absolutely superb! Created by *Golf Digest*, GolfWeb is a paradigm of what a truly great sports Web site can be. When you point your browser at the URL above, you'll see a screen like the one shown in the figure "Welcome to GolfWeb!" Scroll down that screen, and you'll see a button for "About GolfWeb." It's worth clicking on this, since it leads to a page that offers a short but comprehensive overview of the site.

GolfWeb's tag line is "Everything Golf on the World Wide Web!"—and that just may be the case. "GolfWeb is the complete golf information service on the Information Superhighway. No stone will be left unturned, no area left unexplored," say the site's creators.

GolfWeb Coverage and Features

Among the features offered by GolfWeb are "Tournament Reports" with full accounts of each week's PGA, Senior PGA, Nike, European PGA, and LPGA tournaments, updated throughout each tournament. There are sections for statistics, records, and Sony World Rankings. There are press releases; live reports; a GolfWeb library of golf-related books, articles, and reference materials; and "Places to Play," which lets you view listings of courses, resorts, and golf destinations.

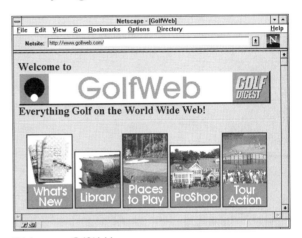

Welcome to GolfWeb!

Naturally, there's a "Pro Shop" where you can buy equipment, clothing, books, videos, and travel services. And there's a "GolfWeb Bulletin Board," which you can use to share your favorite golf story, tip, or recommendation.

There is also a photo section and an area called "OnCourse." "OnCourse" is offered in partnership with the National Golf Course Directory/Data Center. It lets you search a database of about 14,000 courses in the United States and around the world. You can search on the basis of name, zip code, state, and just about any other criteria you can think of.

Once you find a course of interest, you can call up information about it, including the number of holes, fees, guest policy, championship yardage, and more. You can then add your personal comments about the course. And, via the "Arrange a Game" feature, you can post your "availability or willingness to form a game at a particular course."

The people who created GolfWeb have thought of everything! So even if you're not a golfer yourself, it's worth a visit, if only to see what a World Wide Web site can be when it's created by people with both passion and vision.

Travel

37

It *is certainly true that on the Web all points are the same. Physical location does not signify. Yet humankind does not live by the Web and the Net alone. Sometimes you just gotta travel, physically. And when you do, you'll find that it can pay to check the Web before you leave.*

The GNN Travel Page:
http://nearnet.gnn.com/gnn/wic/wics/trav.new.html
The Global Network Navigator, a subsidiary of America Online, offers a master site for travel information. It starts with a greeting screen offering three categories of clickable links. The main heading, "Region & Country Guides," for example, has links for Africa, Western Europe, Canada, world guides, and more. The "Subject Guides" section has

links for adventure travel, guidebooks and tips, maps and weather, and travel narratives, among others. The third category of links is "This Week's Most Popular Travel Sites." When we were there, that list included links to airline and hotel Web sites, and Amtrak schedules.

Weblinks: *http://www.lonelyplanet.com.au/weblinks/weblinks.htm*

Another leading master site for travel information is Weblinks. This site offers a rather eclectic collection of links that includes Amnesty International, Greenpeace, Rainforest Action Network, One World Online, and others. But Weblinks also contains a worldwide directory of tourism offices, and sections called "Local Times Around the World" and "Shoestring Travel" (a collection of tips about traveling on the cheap).

CityLink: *http://banzai.neosoft.com/citylink*

Travel information on the Web is a topic that could easily fill an entire book. Basically, you can assume that tons of information is available for nearly any major international destination or attraction. And if you can't find what you're looking for on Weblinks or GNN's travel site, you can most certainly do so using a Web search engine such as Infoseek, WebCrawler, or Yahoo!.

Since we've only got a single chapter to work with, however, we decided to concentrate on U.S. cities. There are at least two master sites you can go to for travel information organized by city—CityLink and CityNet. The main difference is that CityNet also includes non-U.S. cities.

You can reach CityLink via the URL shown above. But we got there by clicking on the hot link on the GNN travel page. Once at CityLink, we saw a list of the 50 states, plus Washington, D.C., and the U.S. Virgin Islands.

CityLink also has a search feature, so we looked for "Bucks County, Pennsylvania." A page appeared, headed by a picture of a house in Washington Crossing Historic Park (one that we have visited many times). The hypertext highlighted, among other things, attractions, shopping, restaurants, lodging, the local Philadelphia forecast, and maps of Bucks County and the surrounding area.

We clicked on "Restaurants" and were presented with an alphabetical list of restaurants, most of whose names we recognized. So far so good.

The Koblas Currency Converter

Both the GNN and the Weblinks sites offer a hot link to David Koblas's Currency Converter. (The URL is complex, so go to one of these master sites and click on "Koblas Currency Converter.")

By default, the page comes up with the heading "The week's currency rates (one US dollar equals)." An alphabetical list of country names and numbers follows, starting with Argentina and running through Venezuela. You can click on the country name and both the heading and the numbers will change.

So if you want to know the exchange rate for, say, the Japanese yen, click on "Japan." Truly neat.

What was not so good was the small amount of information that appeared when we clicked on a given restaurant name. All we got was its address and phone number. There were no reviews or menu recommendations, no driving directions, and no hours of operation.

This was a major disappointment. But it was typical of the wide variations in quality and completeness you'll find among travel-oriented Web sites. CityLink had nothing to do with the Bucks County Web page—it merely provided a pointer to that page, which was created by someone else.

CityLink (and CityNet) also provide links to other sites that prove to be quite impressive, offering nicely formatted information, such as local government contacts for particular services; lengthy reviews of area restaurants; details about museums, churches, and public schools; and movie listings.

CityNet: *http://www.city.net*

The point is that when it comes to travel, the quality of the information you encounter varies widely. At this writing, you can't count on anything. The Web is not *Travel & Leisure* or *Condé Nast Traveler*, reputable magazines that can be held accountable for what they publish. So our advice, as always, is to be skeptical. But don't let that stop you from taking a look. You just might click into something really good.

That's what we did on CityNet, a site that covers not only the United States but also Germany, Canada, France, and other countries.

We went to the site and searched for Louisville, Kentucky. This produced a page with menu items that included "City Guides," "Food and Drink," and "General Information."

We clicked on the "Food and Drink" option and were treated to an annotated list of restaurants prepared by Robin Garr, former food and wine critic for the *Louisville Courier-Journal*. The restaurant listings included stars for ratings and dollar signs for relative cost. Plus, the section let us opt to select restaurants by type instead of channeling us into the complete list. Restaurant types included barbecue and down-home, bistros, brew pubs, deluxe and four-star, Italian, and more.

The main drawback to CityNet at this writing is that it is not even remotely comprehensive. There was no listing for Bucks County, Pennsylvania, for example, though Lancaster and Berks Counties were covered. There was no entry for New Hope, Pennsylvania (a popular tourist destination), though Jim Thorpe, a tiny town we visit each year to cut our Christmas tree, had an entry. (It wasn't a very impressive entry, but it was there.)

The bottom line, then, is this: The Web has a tremendous amount of very useful travel-related information, but its quality, comprehensiveness, and depth can be spotty. It probably always will be. That's why your best bet is to start with master sites like those we've profiled here. If nothing else, it's easier than spending a lot of time preparing a precise Infoseek or other search engine query. And it will probably lead quickly to satisfactory results.

The Web Browser Cookbook

The *Information Superhighway metaphor for the Internet wore out its welcome with us long ago. Yet, the best way to describe what we're going to teach you here really is how to "drive" a Web browser. Not just* navigate, *but* drive—*as in putting in the clutch, shifting gears, and stepping on the gas. You will find it an enjoyable, even exhilarating, experience.*

The first graphical Web browser was Mosaic. Shortly after it appeared, the team that created it left to form a company called Netscape Communications and to develop a browser called Netscape Navigator (or just Netscape for short). The company's mascot, Mozilla, derives its name from the phrase "Mosaic Killer."

Both CompuServe and Microsoft's Internet Explorer use a version of Mosaic to give subscribers access to the Web. Prodigy and Delphi use Netscape Navigator itself for that purpose, as do about 89 percent of all Web surfers. The Netscape/Mosaic way of doing things holds such a dominant position that you can assume that your browser, whether it's the one provided by America Online or some other company, will offer the same set of essential features.

And in any case, you can almost certainly use Netscape Navigator or another browser of your choice with *any* Internet connection. Which is to say, you can use Netscape Navigator to browse the Web with your AOL or CompuServe connection or with your connection to Netcom and many other Internet Service Providers. (See the sidebar "Using the Windows Browser of Your Choice" for more information.)

It's important to note that the velocity of change in the Web browser field is breathtaking. Hardly a day goes by without the appearance of new features, new proposed standards, and new versions of browser programs. So until things settle down, there's not much point in mastering some advanced feature that may disappear in the next version of your browser program. Your best bet is to focus on the basics, which is exactly what we're going to do here.

Three Steps to Learning to Drive

Naturally, the very first step in using a browser program is getting it installed in the first place. Of necessity, we must assume that the online system or Internet Service Provider you are using has taken care of this. They should have provided you with the software, instructions on how to install it, and a telephone number for customer support (should you run into problems).

We'll pick things up at the point where your browser is installed and tested—so you know that it works. And we'll limit the focus to the most crucial settings or techniques.

Our goal is to make you as competent and comfortable a Web user as possible. We'd much rather you had fun on the Web than spend time mastering the minutiae of any Web browser program. After all, there are entire books devoted to Mosaic, Netscape, and other browsers.

You'll find that the Netscape Handbook, available free of charge from the Netscape Web site, is particularly helpful. It covers both the Windows and Macintosh versions of the program and may even eliminate the need to spend money on a special browser book. At this writing, the location to check is:
http://home.netscape.com/eng/mozilla/2.0/handbook/index.html.

So, with your browser up and running, here are the three main areas we'll focus on:

1. Preparing Your Browser

2. "Driving" Your Browser

3. Tips, Tricks, Mail, and Newsgroups

Using the Windows Browser of Your Choice

The trick for using the browser of your choice under Windows is based on obtaining and installing the version of the file WINSOCK.DLL and the companion dialer program required by your chosen system.

WINSOCK.DLL files act as go-betweens. Each summons its companion dialing program and orders it to dial the phone number you have specified and log you on to a system using the name and password you have supplied to the dialing program. WINSOCK.DLL establishes the connection using the necessary protocol, and then it turns to Netscape, Mosaic, or any other Winsock-compliant program and says, "Okay, who wants to connect to the Net?"

Prodigy has already converted to using Netscape.

If you're a CompuServe user who accesses the system via WinCIM and NetLauncher (CompuServe's Spry Mosaic program), then you already have the necessary WINSOCK.DLL file and dialer program. Using a browser like Netscape could be a simple matter of going to the Netscape home page and downloading a copy. (That page's URL is **http://home.netscape.com**.) The place to look for hands-on information about using other browsers is CompuServe's Net-Launcher support forum (**go nlsupport**).

If you're an America Online subscriber, things are even easier. That's because AOL has introduced a Windows feature dedicated to helping you use Netscape Navigator with its service. Just key in Control-K to bring up the Keyword prompt and type in **Netscape**. You'll see a screen that will not only tell you exactly what

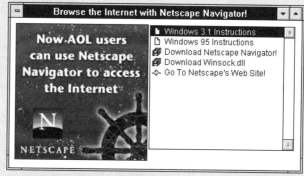

AOL supports Netscape for Windows!

to do but will also provide you with a copy of Netscape for your version of Windows.

Typically, you will want to rename the copy of WINSOCK.DLL supplied by CompuServe, America Online, Netcom, or any other Internet Service Provider to something like OLDSOCK.DLL, and then install the Web browser and version of WINSOCK.DLL and its dialer you want to use.

The main thing to remember is that you can almost always use the Web browser software of your choice with any online system or Internet Service Provider.

Preparing Your Browser

Most browser programs are set to take you to a particular Web location automatically as soon as you click on the browser icon. Let's assume that you've activated Netscape and are now logged on to the Netscape Communications home page. A welcome screen will appear.

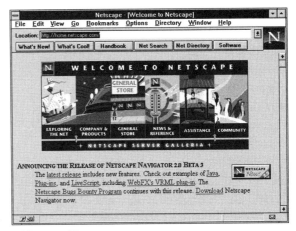

Welcome to Netscape.

If this is your first time on the Web, go have some fun. Click away to your heart's content, letting curiosity be your guide. But one of these days you will want to take the time to prepare your browser. A few easy steps will pay big dividends as you cruise the Web.

Here we'll focus on the following:

- Setting your cache size
- Specifying how often your browser should "verify documents"
- Setting your browser's e-mail and newsgroup features
- Setting up your helper applications

So let's do it!

Setting Your Cache Size

1. Click on "Options" in the menu bar and then on "Network Preferences" on the menu that will drop down. Notice the folder tabs across the screen that appears, starting with "Cache" and ending with "Proxies."

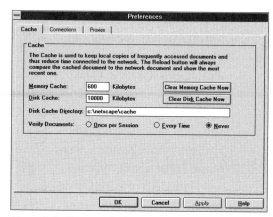

Network Preferences: Cache.

2. You won't have to worry about the "Connections" or the "Proxies" settings unless you are hooked into a local area network (LAN). If that's the case, your office's system administrator is the person to see.

3. All users should home in on the "Cache" settings, especially the "Disk Cache" setting. The version of Netscape Navigator we are using defaults to a disk cache of 5,000 kilobytes, which is to say, 5 megabytes. If you have enough available disk space, you should probably change this to at least 10,000 kilobytes (10 megabytes).

Why? Well, have you ever noticed that when you go to a Web site the *second* time, the graphics and text seem to appear a lot faster than they did on your first visit? The reason is that your browser is probably designed to capture and record in your computer's hard drive cache the text and images it has received from every site you visit.

So when you return to that site, your browser checks that disk cache to see if the images and text that correspond to that site are already on your hard drive. If so, the browser puts them on your screen from disk, which is a heck of a lot faster than ordering a remote site to send them over the Internet connection.

In general, the bigger the disk cache, the better—particularly if you frequently return to the same group of sites. That's why we recommend setting your browser's disk cache to 10 megabytes or more, if you can afford it.

The only drawback to setting up a large cache, aside from the disk space it consumes, is that your browser may perform cache maintenance by deleting older files each time you exit. Often that can take a moment or two, causing you to wonder "What on earth is going on?" as you watch the light on your hard drive flicker.

4. As for "Memory Cache," we recommend leaving it at 600 kilobytes for the time being. No matter how much RAM you've got, memory is always in demand. If you've got a 10-millisecond or faster hard drive, you'll probably see the cached pages reappear fast enough without devoting more RAM to the memory cache. If not, feel free to experiment with a higher number.

Verifying Documents

As you can see in the middle of the figure "Network Preferences: Cache" on page 204, there are three "Verify Documents" "radio buttons" that let you tell Netscape how to handle pages (or documents) stored in your cache. Here's what they mean:

- The "Once per Session" setting tells the program to get a fresh copy of a given page the first time you visit a site in each online session. If you go back to the site or back to a page during the session, Netscape will use the copy of the page stored in the cache instead of downloading it again.
- The "Every Time" setting means that the program should always download the page, rather than attempting to retrieve it from the cache.
- The "Never" setting means that the program should never attempt to download the page. Instead, it should always show you the copy that is stored in the cache whenever you return to that location.

The setting that's best for you depends on how you use the Web, but this is what we recommend:

1. Start by choosing the "Never" setting. The reason is speed. If you set your disk cache for 10 megabytes and "Verify Documents" for "Never," you will have a much more enjoyable Web experience once you begin to revisit sites that you like.

2. Should you click on a link on a page that has been retrieved from the cache and find that the link no longer exists, simply click on "View" in the menu bar of the main browser window and then click on "Reload." Or just click the Reload button atop the browser screen. The Reload command will cause the site to send you a fresh copy of the page. The Reload command thus puts you in control.

3. To finish with the screen in the figure "Network Preferences: Cache," click on "OK." All Preferences settings are saved this way. (Clicking on "Save Options" in the Options drop-down menu has no effect on Preferences settings.)

Mail and News Preferences

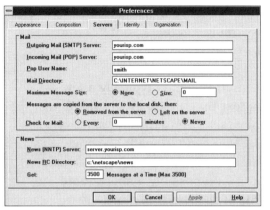

Specifying mail and news server addresses.

If you're using a browser with America Online, Prodigy, Compu-Serve, Delphi, or some other big consumer service, you probably won't have to think about configuring your software to work with Usenet newsgroups or Internet mail. That's because those systems typically offer built-in newsgroup and e-mail features.

But if you're using an Internet Service Provider (ISP), you may have to tell your browser about the "server computers" you want it to use and about your identity. Here's how:

1. Click on "Options" and then on "Mail and News Preferences." Notice the names on the folder tabs across the top of the screen.

2. Click on "Servers" and make sure the blanks have been filled in with the domain name of your Internet Service Provider (the name to the right of the @ sign in your e-mail address). In this example, we've used **yourisp.com** as the address for both outgoing and incoming mail.

3. For "Pop User Name" (POP stands for Post Office Protocol), key in the name to the left of the @ sign in your e-mail account. For this example, we used **smith**.

4. Leave everything else as it is and go down to "News (NNTP) Server." What's needed here is the address of the server Netscape should contact whenever you want to read Usenet newsgroups. You'll need to get this address from your Internet Service Provider if you don't have it already. (Check the materials you received when you signed up for your Internet account, or call your service provider's customer or technical support department.)

5. Click on the "OK" button and then on the "Identity" file folder tab near the top of the "Preferences" screen. That will take you to a screen that will request your name, e-mail address, reply-to-e-mail address, and signature file.

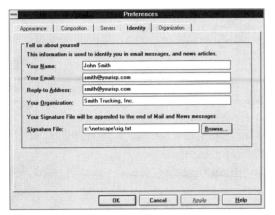

Your e-mail identity screen.

6. A "signature file" is typically a few lines of text that a mail program automatically tacks on to the end of every message you send. Usually, it contains your land address, voice and fax numbers, and possibly a short quote or words of wisdom that appeal to you. The key word here is *short!* In fact, if your signature file is longer than four lines, Netscape will notify you of that fact. However, the program will still accept the file you specify, regardless of length.

7. Prepare your signature file with a text editor or with your word processor, taking care to save it as plain ASCII text.

8. Key in the name of the file in the Preferences Identity screen, and Netscape will automatically attach it to any e-mail you send.

Setting Up Helper Applications

Before moving on to learning how to drive a browser, we need to say a word or two about "helper applications." Click on "Options" and then "General Preferences" and then on the file folder tab labeled "Helpers" to set up helper applications in Netscape.

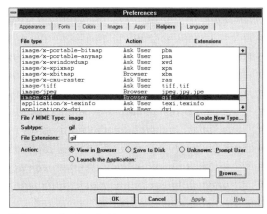

Helper applications in Netscape.

A major goal of hardware and software manufacturers, Internet companies, and nontech companies is for you to be able to click on an image or sound icon and have your screen automatically come to life with full-motion video, sound, and photographic-quality still images. Unfortunately, things are still pretty kludgey.

There are as yet no universally accepted standards for anything. There are dozens of formats for graphics and sound files, for example. And no browser can be expected to incorporate programming to display or play all of them. So the burden is on you.

It's up to you to locate, say, a viewer program that can display several flavors of .TIF (Tagged Image Format) files, copy it to your hard disk, and then tell your browser that it should call that program whenever it sees a .TIF file coming in.

The whole thing depends on formally *associating* a given file type, as determined by the file name extension, with a given program. Thus, if you have told Netscape or another browser that whenever it is sent a file with a name that ends in .TIF or .BMP, it should feed that file to a program called LVIEW.EXE, you should be able to see the file onscreen after it arrives.

You can do the same thing with sound files and with movie files in the MPEG or Apple QuickTime format. And why stop there? By associating the file extension .ZIP with a program called PKZIP.EXE, you can tell Netscape to automatically "unzip" (decompress) such a file once it is received.

The Web Browser Cookbook

Real Help with Helper Applications

This kind of inconvenience isn't going to last. At this writing, there is already a movement toward more convenient "plug-in programs"— programs that will tell themselves and Netscape about each other. Plug-ins make it easy to add to Netscape's capabilities.

Netscape Communications, in fact, offers a product called the Netscape Power Pack for $54.95. The modules include Netscape Smart-Marks for managing your bookmarks, Netscape Chat, Adobe Acrobat Reader, Apple QuickTime, and RealAudio Player. For more information go to **http://home.netscape.com/comprod/power_pack_summary.html**.

Eventually everyone will agree on universal standards for graphics, sound, and video, and the whole helper program approach will go away. The code needed to deal with such files will be built into the browser software, made available as an easy-to-use plug-in, or be transmitted directly to you via the Net as explained in the Java sidebar on pages 211–212. In the meantime, we have some pointed advice:

1. When you FTP a file or otherwise ask a server to send you a file, and Netscape tells you "No viewer has been configured for this file type," tell your browser to *save the file to disk*. You might even want to use the screen shown on page 209 to tell Netscape to save *every* file type to disk without asking you.

2. Once the file is on disk, you can run the necessary decompression program or viewing or sound-playing helper application against it. If you like it, keep it. If not, delete it.

3. If you're going to decompress an archive, first copy the archive into its own separate directory, like \TEMP or \JUNK or whatever. Otherwise you'll end up with a complete jumble of files on your disk. Before long, you won't know which file goes with which program.

4. Where can you find the relevant helper programs? Windows and DOS users can find many of them in the Internet Toolkit and Gloss-brenner's Choice Appendix. But Macintosh users and everyone else can also find them on the Net, on the Big Three systems, and on bulletin boards (see Chapter 26 for locations offering free software).

What's All the Fuss About Java?

It's almost impossible these days to encounter a computer magazine, or even a general-interest newspaper, that doesn't have something to say about Java, the programming language introduced by Sun Microsystems in January, 1996. For the record, HotJava is the name of the Sun Web browser that incorporates support for the Java language. But Netscape signed a deal with Sun early on, so starting with Netscape Navigator 2.0, Java support has been included.

So what's the big deal? The big deal is that Java eliminates the need for helper applications when you're browsing the Web. If you use a Java-enabled browser and you sign on to a Java-enabled site, you can click on an icon for an animated image or video clip and it will simply *appear* on your screen, possibly with stereo sound in the background.

Java makes possible *seamless* multimedia interactions with the Web, as opposed to the situation today that requires you to download a file and tell your browser which helper application you want it to use to play the sound or display the image or the video clip.

Java can do this because it is a full-blown programming language based more or less on C++. This gives Web-page creators the power to send you not only image, sound, and video files, but also the *actual program* you need to view, listen to, or play each one. For example, the programming needed to display a graphic file called for by a particular HTML Web page can be embedded in the page itself, so that it is downloaded to your system when you go to that page.

Your Java-enabled Web browser recognizes the programming as programming and, in effect, runs the program. No need to worry about whether the graphic is a .GIF, .TIF, or .PCX file or about which viewer program should be associated with it. The graphic could be in a completely unique format and it wouldn't matter, because the programming needed to view that graphic is supplied automatically as soon as you go to that Web page.

Of course, as of early 1996, everything is in the beta-test stage, from Java itself to the next version of Netscape. As you read this, things may have solidified. But at this point, you can benefit from Java only if you are running in full 32-bit mode, which means at least Windows 95 for most users. (Win32s, the add-on that lets Windows 3.x access some 32-bit features in 386 chips and above, does not qualify.)

Finally, the most intriguing (or crazy) implication of the Java-Netscape-Web connection is that it might somehow put Microsoft out of business. Publications as diverse as *Business Week* and *InfoWorld* have suggested as much. It has been pointed out that the Java language is powerful enough for someone to use for creating a spreadsheet, word processor, or other application program. After all, many best-selling programs these days are written in C++.

And, since Java programming comes across as plain ASCII text, just like an HTML Web page, a Java-enabled browser on any kind of computer can run those programs. (Remember what we've said earlier in this book about ASCII text being the common language of online ▶

What's All the Fuss About Java? *(cont.)*

▶ communications.) So someone could write a program in Java that both Windows and Macintosh users could run via their Java-enabled Web browsers. No need for a Mac version and a Windows version. Do a Java version, and you've covered both platforms.

The key, of course, is the Java-enabled browser the user runs. So the notion has been floated that in the future, it will be the Web browser program, not Windows or System 7, that controls the desktop. In the future, you won't buy Microsoft Word or WordPerfect. Nope, when you want to write a letter, you'll just sign on to the Net with your browser and download a Java-based word processing "applet" (a tiny application) into memory, create and save your text to disk, and sign off. The word processing applet will then disappear.

Pardon us for being skeptical. On the one hand, we know that precisely this kind of process has been taking place on local area networks for years, where users download temporary copies of programs from the network server for a current job. On the other hand, we cannot see how anyone in business would tolerate having their mission-critical software located on a third-party server and delivered on an ad hoc basis.

We may well be shooting ourselves in the foot, but, in our opinion, the notion that Java and Netscape are somehow going to topple Microsoft has more to do with envy-driven wishful thinking than it does with bare-metal reality. After all, as we have said for years, the greatest cost in personal computing is not the hardware or the software—it's the time required to learn to use the stuff effectively.

People don't want a word processor du jour downloaded from the Net. They want what they have learned how to use. Then again, anyone who predicts anything with certainty in this business clearly doesn't know what he or she is talking about. So if you see us limping around with a bum foot, you'll know we were wrong. But, at this point, we don't think so.

In our opinion, Java and the plug-ins offered in the Netscape Power Pack will make possible seamless sound, graphics, and video on the Web. They will eliminate the need to concern yourself with helper applications. But we would be very surprised if things went much further than that. After all, just because it's *possible* to download a spreadsheet program written in Java to be run on a user's system does not mean that it is *desirable* to do so.

Still, if you have a Java-enabled browser and you want to visit some Java sites, you could start with a Web search using the word "Java." Or, you might try one or more of these locations:

*   **http://www.dimensionx.com/dnx**
*   **http://www.gamelan.com/Gamelan.programming.html**
*   **http://www.javasoft.com**
*   **http://rendezvous.com/java/hierarchy/index.html**
*   **http://www.rpi.edu/^decemj/works/java/bib.html**
*   **http://www.science.wayne.edu/^joey/java.html**

"Driving" Your Browser

Driving a Web browser isn't difficult. But you'll need a starting location and some basic commands. Quite understandably, companies like America Online, Netscape, and CompuServe have set their browsers to start you off at their own home pages. But you can alter this default by using one of the "Preferences"-style setup menus.

In Netscape, for example, clicking on "Options," "General Preferences," and "Appearance" takes you to a screen that lets you specify your starting home page location. Just key in the desired URL address and click on "OK" to save the setting.

Probably the most important "driving" command of all is learning to hit the Escape key or click on the Stop icon in the toolbar. Both actions have the same effect—they tell the Web site to *stop* sending you graphics and text. Once you've stopped the loading of a Web page, your browser will be able to give you its full attention, allowing you to tell it to go someplace else or do something else.

The Web Browser Cookbook

Hypertext Links and Getting Back

Regardless of your particular "home" location, once you're there, the steps are the same:

1. You can click on the icons, buttons, or color-highlighted words of text you see on your screen. The latter are the hypertext links we've spoken about elsewhere. Each click will take you someplace else.

2. Alternately, you can click on the box labeled "Netsite" or "Location" (or something similar) that you'll find near the top of the screen. Then type in the URL of the place you want to visit.

3. Deeper and deeper you'll drive your browser into the Web. And you'll always end up someplace. The question is: How do you get back to where you started? And how do you return to a particular page you encountered along the way?

4. The answer: Just click the "Back" button. That will take you back to the page you just left. And from there you can click "Back" again to return to the page before that or click on "Go" and then on "Back" on the menu that will drop down.

   If you are visiting a site that uses Netscape 2.0's "Frames" feature, don't use the "Back" button. Instead, hold down your right mouse button within the frame and a pop-up menu will give you the choice of going "Back in Frame" or "Forward in Frame." If you're a Macintosh user, just put the cursor in the target frame and hold down your mouse button.

5. Fortunately, browser programs keep track of where you've been. So you do not have to back out of a location sequentially. If you've visited ten pages in your current session, and if you then click on "Go," you'll see a list of each location you've already visited. Click on the entry you want, and you will be whisked to it as if you had booked a direct flight.

A Bit Beyond the Basics: Bookmarks

Now you know how to tell your browser to go to any of the sites discussed in this book. Just mouse up to the box labeled "Location" or "Netsite" (or something similar) and key in one of the URLs you've seen in this book. It could start with **http://** to go to a Web site, or with **news:** to go to a newsgroup, or it might start with something else.

You know how to go back to the last location you visited and how to go directly to any other location you visited this session. The trouble is, all of that goes away once you close this session.

Wouldn't it be neat if you could record a location's URL on a list and save the list to disk so that it would be there for you the *next* time you loaded your browser?

That's what features like Netscape's Bookmarks, AOL's Favorite Places, and CompuServe's HotSpots are all about:

1. If you're on the Net or the Web and you come across a really interesting site—a site you think you will probably want to go back to in the future—all you've got to do to record its location is to add it to your list of Bookmarks or Favorite Places or HotSpots.

2. The site's name and address will be recorded in a file on disk, eliminating the need for you to ever key in its official URL address again.

3. The next time you want to visit a given site, load your browser and click on "Bookmarks" or your program's equivalent, and find the site name on the list that will appear.

And speaking of Bookmarks, you should know that Netscape Communications introduced a new feature called SmartMarks late in 1995 as part of its Power Pack offering. This add-on comes with 300 preloaded Bookmarks, including links to Yahoo!'s most popular Web sites. SmartMarks lets you edit, prune, and organize your Bookmarks list.

But it also lets you do *Bookmark monitoring.* Just tag the Bookmark of a particular site and Netscape SmartMarks will periodically check it for changes. When a change is detected, the program will notify you of that fact and suggest that you revisit the site. For more information, call 800-638-7483 or visit **http://home.netscape.com**.

Bookmark Organizing

It has been suggested by *InfoWorld*'s Stewart Alsop Jr. and others that the future lies with Web browser bookmarks. Those who provide the bookmark files rule the Web, in other words. Well, maybe. With over 400,000 Web sites out there, and heaven only knows how many Gopher, Telnet, and FTP sites, it's just possible that someone who can supply a prepackaged file of bookmarks could do quite well.

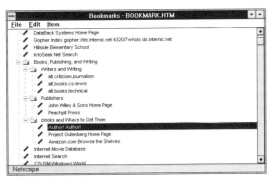

An arrangement of Bookmarks.

Imagine: Instead of getting those packages of coupons in the mail every other day, you get a disk containing a file of Web bookmarks. Add the file to your browser's list, and you're only a click or two away from the Web page put up by your local carpet cleaner or Chinese restaurant. Each page, of course, would contain valuable coupons or possibly that day's special offer.

This is such an obvious application that we can say it is almost certainly going to happen. (We want to be a little less than forceful here, in case we need our other foot!)

In the meantime, you should know that Web browsers often include modules for managing, pruning, and arranging Bookmarks (or Favorite Places or HotSpots or whatever).

With Netscape, for example, you can create a Bookmark list. Here's how it works:

1. We should explain that the kind of display you see in the figure won't appear until you have added quite a few Bookmarks to your list. When you see a line for "More Bookmarks" at the bottom of the Netscape Bookmarks menu, you will know that you've assembled a sizable number.

2. Click on "More Bookmarks" in Netscape and you will be taken to a screen that offers you the chance to organize your collected Bookmarks by topic or folder. We won't attempt a complete tutorial, but we'll show you the basic steps for organizing your Bookmarks under Netscape.

3. Mouse to a point on the list, click to mark the spot, and then mouse up to and click on "Item" and then "Insert Folder."

4. You can call the folder anything you like. Then you can click on and drag any Bookmark on the list into the folder you've created.

5. Finally, to change the name of a Bookmark entry, select it and click on your *right* mouse button to get to "Properties," or click on the entry once to select it and then click on "Item" and then on "Properties."

Saving a Web Page

The last basic skill that any browser user needs is to be able to save to disk what appears on the screen. Start by practicing what we've told you so far. Select a site mentioned in this book. Go there, then go someplace else by clicking on a hot link, then go back to the first site. Add one or more sites to your Bookmarks or Favorite Places list. Then use those features to return to the sites.

Convince yourself, in other words, that you know how to drive in forward and reverse and you know how to easily return to places that you like. You now know how to surf the Web. You can get where you want to go.

Now for the challenge of *saving* what you find. This is easy to do. The key is to remember that the typical Web page physically consists of *several* different files:

- The master HTML text file contains all of the words you see and all the codes that say which size of type should be used when displaying each word.
- The inline graphics files each contain a separate image. The master HTML file includes instructions that tell your browser which graphic file to display and where to display it.

Thus, while what you see on your screen may appear to be a single, smoothly scrolling file, in reality its components are no more unified than the various text and image files you pulled together with your word processor when you prepared, say, your department's latest proposal or quarterly report.

With that in mind, here's how to save a Web site:

1. First of all, be sure to wait for the entire file to arrive before saving or printing it. Wait until you see a phrase like "Document Done" in the lower left portion of your browser screen before you take action.

2. The quickest, easiest way to preserve a Web page is to simply print it. Clicking on "File" and then on "Print" should do the job in most cases. Or, if you're using Netscape, just click the "Print" button.

3. To save the file to disk, click on "File" and then "Save As" to tell your browser to write the page to your disk using the name you specify. That will get you the HTML or plain text file if you make sure the file-name ends with ".txt." But there will be no graphic images. (You can later view the HTML file in Netscape by clicking on "File" and then "Open File.")

4. To save the graphics to disk, move your mouse to each graphic image and click the mouse button (that's the *right* mouse button for Windows users). If you're using Netscape, you will then be prompted for the name you want to use when saving the image to disk. Not all browsers offer this feature.

5. You can save the graphic files under whichever names you want. Then, once you're offline, you can go back and make your file names square with the file names called for by the HTML file, either by editing the HTML file or by changing the file names of the graphic images.

As you may recall, all of the HTML and graphic file components of the page you want to save are probably in your cache. But they are a hassle to find. Saving Web pages and images this way will take a lot less time in the long run.

There is enough to be said about Netscape Navigator and other Web browsers to fill many books. We don't have that kind of space here. But we are pleased to be able to share a few pointers that will help you cut through all the irrelevant information you're likely to encounter about using a browser.

Starting Multiple Sessions

In Netscape, if you mouse up to "File" and click, the first selection on the drop-down menu is "New Web Browser." If you click on that selection, you will start a *second* copy of Netscape, which you can point at any location you please.

This is something that is hard for old online hands like us to accept, but it's true, thanks to the miracle of networking. Imagine: You start your first copy of Netscape and tell it to go to a site and begin downloading a very large file. The download might take as long as 20 minutes. But you don't have to remain idle. Simply click on "File" and then on "New Web Browser" to start a second copy of Netscape, and use it to continue surfing the Web while the first copy of Netscape continues downloading in the background.

The Netscape documentation doesn't say anything about how many copies can be open at the same time. We've opened as many as four with no protest from Netscape itself. Certainly the more powerful your computer, the better your results are likely to be when running multiple sessions at the same time.

Stopping a Download

Another good tip is to hit your Escape key whenever you want to tell your browser to stop accepting data from a remote site. This is the same as mousing up to the top of the screen and clicking on the Stop button, but it's much faster.

Online Support and Answers

If the documentation offered on the Netscape home page isn't enough for you, try one or both of the two online venues for Netscape support: Usenet newsgroups and Netscape User Groups (NUGgies). They are both good sources of additional information.

1. Point your browser at **news:comp.infosystems.www.browsers.ms-windows**, or use Netscape's built-in newsreader to access this newsgroup, which is one of the main exchange points for questions and answers about Windows browsers. Scan the messages, and if you don't find an answer to your particular question, post your query and check back a while later.

2. You can also tap into the Netscape User Groups (NUGgies) created by Netscape Communications. You'll find them in the "Community" section of the Netscape home page, or just point your browser at **http://www.netscape.com/commun/netscape_user_groups.html**.
At this writing, there are groups devoted to the following:
- Test Driving
- Server Applications
- General Topics
- Security
- Netscape Navigator
- Netscape Servers

E-Mail via Netscape

Electronic mail via Netscape—there's an interesting idea, one that gained weight only with Netscape Navigator 2.x, because previous versions of the program could send but not receive e-mail. It's not likely to be a factor for America Online, CompuServe, or Prodigy subscribers, since each of those systems has its own built-in e-mail feature. But Netscape-based or browser-based e-mail could be very important to anyone who accesses the Net using an Internet Service Provider (ISP).

For example, when we signed up with our ISP some time ago, we were given an entire toolbox of shareware programs, including not only Netscape and Winsock, but also the Eudora mail program, a Telnet program, an FTP program, and so on. Today, all of those Internet features can be tapped from within Netscape Navigator and most other modern browsers.

This is good, because it means you never have to leave, load, and learn to use a separate program. It is less than good, however, if your e-mail or newsgroup-reading needs go beyond the basics. No software product can be all things to all people.

Still, we think you will find that the e-mail features built into Netscape Navigator Version 2.x are well worth a look. Here are the steps to follow:

1. If you click on "Options," then "Mail," then "News Preferences," you will be taken to a screen that lets you tell Netscape to automatically check for mail every *x* number of minutes.

2. Click on the little Envelope icon in the lower right of the Netscape screen, and you will be taken directly to the e-mail feature. Alternately, you can click on "Window" and then on "Netscape Mail" to get there.

3. You'll find that the e-mail features built into Netscape 2.x rival the popular Eudora stand-alone e-mail program. You can attach files to messages, create an address book, automatically add a signature file, encode text (using ROT-13), and perform all of the other main functions of a dedicated Internet e-mail program. Netscape may not offer everything you need, but it is no "poor cousin" add-on. In other words, it is well worth investing the time needed to learn how to use it. You may find that it can satisfy all of your e-mail needs.

4. Don't forget that you can get the basic instructions on how to use Netscape's e-mail and other features by going to **http://home.netscape.com/eng/mozilla/2.0/handbook/index.html**.

Reading Newsgroups via Netscape

Reading newsgroups with Netscape.

Now let's look at newsgroups. They are not a Web feature, but they hold an incredible wealth of information. Plus, they give you the opportunity to post a question and get an answer.

CompuServe, AOL, and Prodigy have proprietary features for reading Internet newsgroups. But Netscape and other browsers you may encounter also have news-group-reading features. And we're not just talking about the ability offered by all browsers to respond to the **news:** URL. We mean full-blown features that keep track of the groups you have subscribed to and the messages within each group that you have read.

A complete tutorial on using Netscape to tap into Usenet newsgroups is beyond the scope of this book. But, as you will discover, a tutorial is not necessary. All you need are the basic concepts and 15 minutes with a mouse, and you will get the hang of it. Follow these steps:

1. When you click on "Window" and then on "Netscape News" using the menu bar near the top of the screen, you will be taken to a screen that is divided into three parts.

2. The most important phrase on this screen is "News Server" at the top of the window on the left. If you have configured your browser as discussed earlier, you will probably see three News Servers laid out here, the first of which will be the news server maintained by your own ISP.

3. Keep in mind that not all Usenet newsgroup servers offer all news-groups. As the number of newsgroups approaches the 20,000 mark, news "servers" have had to cut back on the number of groups they carry and on the length of time they allow each posting to remain on the system.

4. If you have a SLIP or PPP connection with an ISP, you'll first want to find out about and record which newsgroups your ISP offers. Remember that we told Netscape about our ISP and newsgroups earlier when we set our Mail and News Preferences (see page 207). So start with that. Click on "Window" and then on "Netscape News."

5. Mouse to the left window and click on the plus sign next to your chosen ISP news server's folder icon.

6. Mouse up to the top of the screen and click on "Options." Then click on "Show All Newsgroups" on the drop-down menu that will appear. Your server will transmit the names of all the groups it carries. This can take some time, but the results will be recorded on disk, so you will never have to get the entire list again.

7. Here is the most crucial concept of all, however. The information that gets recorded on disk consists solely of the names and URLs of newsgroups. No actual newsgroup messages are involved. What you've got, in effect, is a map of newsgroups, the details of which will be filled in when you are actually online.

8. To get that map or menu to appear again, sign on to your ISP's system and click on "Window" and then on "Netscape News." Click on the plus sign near the news server of your choice in the left window, which will cause it to turn into a minus sign.

9. Mouse up to "Options," click, and select "Show All Newsgroups." If all goes as planned, this should produce an extensive list of newsgroup names in the left window.

10. You may want to grab the divider that separates the right and left windows and drag it left or right to redistribute screen space between the two windows. You can also grab the bottom divider to change the amount of space at the bottom of the screen for reading messages.

11. Open a newsgroup folder in the left window, select the name of a newsgroup, and double-click. Netscape will then go get the headers of the messages that have been posted to that newsgroup and display them in the right screen.

12. When you click on a message header in the right screen, the message will be retrieved and displayed in the bottom portion of the main screen. In the figure on page 222, we selected the newsgroup **alt.coupons** and clicked on the message "Finding rebate offers." Netscape retrieved the message and displayed it in the lower portion of the screen.

The Most Convenient Way to Read Newsgroups

It's fun to use the techniques outlined here to explore the ever-widening world of Usenet newsgroups. But you may prefer a more direct approach. That's why we like the Lawrence List we told you about in Chapter 19. The Lawrence List gives you not only a newsgroup's name, but also a one-sentence description of what it covers.

To find and read newsgroups on subjects of interest, follow these steps:

1. Get the Lawrence List, search it with your word processor for topics of interest, and write down the names of the relevant newsgroups.

2. You can then go directly to those newsgroups by mousing up to the "Netsite" or "Location" box and keying in the URL. To go directly to the coupons newsgroup, for example, you would key in **news:alt.coupons**. Better still, just cut a URL from the List and paste it into your browser's URL box.

3. The Netscape newsreader will then open, and you'll be able to read the latest messages.

Returning to Favorite Newsgroups

Once you've explored newsgroups, you will undoubtedly find that there are some you want to visit often. You will want, in short, to create a list of favorites. This is very easy. Just follow these steps:

1. "Subscribe" to the group (add it to your list of favorites). Go to the newsgroup following the steps outlined earlier, and when its name appears in the left window of the newsreader, just click on the little box to the right of its name. A pair of blue spectacles will appear in the box, indicating that you have "subscribed."

2. To use your favorites list, load the newsreader and click on "Options." Then click on "Show subscribed newsgroups."

3. Click on "Save Options" to make this a permanent setting. From now on (until you change the setting), you will see in the left window only the newsgroups to which you've subscribed.

4. To access your favorite groups as quickly as possible, set things up this way and then add each newsgroup to your Bookmarks list. Just remember that the URL for newsgroups begins with **news:** (no slashes).

The Internet Toolkit and Glossbrenner's Choice

appendix

Forget the learned essays on the significance of cyberspace. What the World Wide Web and the Internet really mean is "anything you want, whenever you want it." You need a program that will display .GIF graphics files? A tutorial on making the most of Internet newsgroups? A program that will transform UU-encoded text files back into viewable graphic images? No problem! Just check the Net.

But there are, in fact, two problems. First, Internet sites come and go, and the names of specific files change over time. So it is pointless for us to say "Go to site XYZ and download the file called ABC.ZIP." As you read this, the site may no longer exist, and if it does, the file name may have changed to something like "ABC-01P.ZIP."

Second, there's no way to know what you're going to need until you actually need it. For example, a Web page alerts you to a file that contains a marvelous image of a rare butterfly. You opt to download it, only to discover that you can't display the image because it's in .PCX (PC Paintbrush) format. Now you've got to search for and download a viewer program that can handle .PCX files. What a nuisance!

This appendix is designed to eliminate—or at least reduce—such hassles. Certainly we can't anticipate absolutely every need. But with nearly 20 years of online experience, we have a pretty good idea of what most people are likely to require as they wade into cyberspace.

There isn't a file on any of the disks offered here that you can't get online from the Internet, America Online, CompuServe, Prodigy, or a bulletin board system. We know, because that's where we got most of these files ourselves. (Check Chapter 26 of this book for hands-on details about how to obtain free software.)

We've located, tested, and selected the best programs and files for our own use. But it occurred to us that readers might appreciate the opportunity to benefit from our experience, not to mention the convenience of being able to get most of the tools they need from one place. So we've organized the files and programs we use to surf the Net and put them on disks.

The programs and text files contained on these disks are free. But the disks themselves, the postage, and the labor needed to make copies and put them in the mail are not. To cover those costs, we charge $5 per disk.

The Internet Toolkit

We've organized the files into a collection of eight disks we call the Internet Toolkit. Most of the contents of these disks are pure ASCII text files that can be read by users of both Windows/DOS machines and Apple Macintoshes, thanks to Apple's SuperDrive technology. (If your Mac was manufactured after August 1989, it is almost certainly equipped with a SuperDrive capable of reading 1.44-megabyte DOS-formatted disks.)

Here, then, is a quick summary of the disks in the Internet Toolkit and their contents:

Internet World Wide Web Essentials

This disk contains many text files concerning the World Wide Web, including "A Beginner's Guide to HTML" and "A Beginner's Guide to URLs" from the National Center for Supercomputing Applications (NCSA). It also includes three DOS/Windows programs. One is called DE-HTML and is designed to convert any saved HTML file into plain, single-spaced text. The second can convert .AU sound files into the .VOC format used by SoundBlaster-compatible sound cards. The third program, MOZSOCK.DLL, makes it possible to load any Winsock-compatible Windows program *without* automatically dialing the phone and going online. This is especially convenient when you want to use your browser to view saved HTML files without actually making an online connection.

Internet Compression and Conversion Tools (Windows/DOS users only)

This is a collection of all the programs Windows/DOS users need to decompress or dearchive the various files available on the Internet, along with our quick-start guide showing how to use each one. Extraction programs range from those for .ARC and .ARJ files to .ZIP, .Z, and .ZOO. There's even a program to "unstuff" Macintosh-produced .SIT files. This disk also includes a program to deal with UU-encoded binary files—such as the graphic images posted to some newsgroups. Capture the relevant newsgroup messages to disk, making sure that you get all of the parts of the image. Run the UU-CODE program against the captured file to convert the data into .GIF, .PCX, or other files. Then look at the images with Graphic Workshop, Adobe Photoshop, or a similar program.

Internet FTP Essentials

On this disk you'll find Perry Rovers's excellent FAQ on anonymous FTP, along with his list of FTP sites that's about as comprehensive as you can imagine. You will almost certainly be doing your FTPing via your Web browser, but your browser will deploy a thin candy shell over the FTP process. The files on this disk strip away the shell and help you make the most of what's really going on.

Internet Basics

This disk contains some of the best files we've come across to help new users get up and running on the Internet. Included are the famous Yanoff List of recommendations of great Internet sites to explore, a guide to the subject-specific lists of Internet resources available from the University of Michigan Clearinghouse, and a comprehensive list of Internet Service Providers (the POCIA List).

Internet Just the FAQs

Here are some of the best and most useful FAQ (Frequently Asked Question) files on the Internet, covering topics such as compression, graphics, chat (IRC), MUDs (text-based "multiuser dungeon" games), Gopher, and Veronica. In writing this book, we've done our best to make this disk unnecessary. But we'd be the first to acknowledge that no book can cover everything. You'll find details on this disk that we did not have space to present in these pages.

Internet Mailing List Essentials

Newbies can be forgiven for thinking that the Internet begins and ends with the World Wide Web. Indeed, the Web is very much a newcomer itself. Internet mailing lists, in contrast, date to nearly the beginning of the Internet. And we've got to admit that there's something nice about having information on a particular topic automatically appear in your mailbox, instead of having to go out and get it. This two-disk set contains two gigantic lists of Internet and Bitnet mailing lists—the SRI List of Lists and the Publicly Accessible Mailing Lists (PAML) list. For each mailing list, you'll find a description of the list provided by the list's sponsor or creator, as well as information on how to subscribe.

Internet Newsgroup Essentials

Newsgroups are a world unto themselves. Unfortunately, they, too, are being neglected in the current frenzy for the Web. That's a big mistake. This disk includes the famous Lawrence List of newsgroups, all 15,000 to 20,000 of them, each with a witty, one-sentence description. Also included is the ROT-13 program Windows/DOS users need to read some of the raunchier jokes in certain newsgroups.

Glossbrenner's Choice

Your co-authors are crazy about shareware. But, you know, price really isn't the point. The point is artistry. Big companies rarely produce great software. That's because great software is always the product of a vision held either by one person or by a very small group of people. Great software is great art! And no committee or workgroup has ever created anything that could be mistaken for art.

In our opinion, the shareware on the following three disks could not be mistaken for anything but art:

Encryption Tools

Although the chances of it happening are slim, someone who really wants to read your electronic mail can probably find a way to do so. But should you ever want to encrypt a text or binary file so that *no one* can read it without the decoding "key," then this is the disk for you. Among other things, it includes Philip Zimmermann's famous Pretty Good Privacy program that's driving the FBI nuts!

Graphic Workshop for DOS

This program by Steven Rimmer is designed to help DOS users deal with nearly any kind of graphics file. No fuss, no muss. Get to DOS, key in **gws**, and you're ready to view, print, crop, scale, and convert to and from virtually every graphics file format going, including .BMP, .EPS, .GEM/.IMG, .GIF, .JPG (JPEG), .IFF/.LBM, .MAC, .PCX, .RLE, and .TIFF, among others.

Graphic Workshop for Windows

GWS for Windows does everything the DOS version does and more. It presents you with a thumbnail screen that shows you quick renditions of each graphic file on your disk. This saves time since it ensures that you will always load just the image you want. Use your Web browser to download a graphics file and save it to disk. Then look at it, manipulate it, or print it with this program.

Order Form

You can use the order form on the next page (or a photocopy) to order the disks described here, as well as a selection of books by Alfred and Emily Glossbrenner. Or you may simply write your request on a piece of paper and send it to us.

We accept American Express, MasterCard, Visa, and checks or money orders made payable to Glossbrenner's Choice (U.S. funds drawn on a U.S. bank, or international money orders). For additional information, write or call:

Glossbrenner's Choice
699 River Road
Yardley, PA 19067-1965
215-736-1213 (voice)
215-736-1031 (fax)
books@mailback.com (information about Glossbrenner books)
alfred@delphi.com or **70065.745@compuserve.com** (all other correspondence)

Glossbrenner's Choice Order Form
for Readers of *The Little Web Book*

Name _____

Address _____

City _____ State _____ Zip _____

Province/Country _____ Phone _____

The Internet Toolkit:

___ Internet World Wide Web Essentials
___ Internet Compression and Conversion Tools
___ Internet FTP Essentials
___ Internet Basics
___ Internet Just the FAQs
___ Internet Mailing List Essentials (Disk 1 of 2)
___ Internet Mailing List Essentials (Disk 2 of 2)
___ Internet Newsgroup Essentials

Glossbrenner's Choice:

___ Encryption Tools
___ Graphic Workshop for DOS
___ Graphic Workshop for Windows

        ___ Total number of disks (3.5-inch, DOS formatted, 1.44MB) ....($5 per disk)   _____

                        Shipping ($3 to U.S. addresses or $5 outside the U.S.)   _____

                                                        TOTAL FOR DISKS: _____

Glossbrenner Publications: (prices include shipping)

___ *The Complete Modem Handbook*, MIS:Press ....($38) _____
___ *Finding a Job on the Internet*, McGraw-Hill ....($19) _____
___ *Internet 101: A College Student's Guide*, McGraw-Hill ....($23) _____
___ *The Little Online Book*, Peachpit Press ....($20) _____
___ *The Little Web Book*, Peachpit Press ....($21) _____
___ *Making Money on the Internet*, McGraw-Hill ....($23) _____
___ *Online Resources for Business*, John Wiley & Sons ....($28) _____

                                                TOTAL FOR BOOKS: _____

                                                        SUBTOTAL: _____

                        Pennsylvania residents, please add 6% sales tax   _____

                                        GRAND TOTAL ENCLOSED: _____

Payment: ☐ Check or Money Order payable to **Glossbrenner's Choice**
              ☐ Amex/MC/Visa _____ Exp ____/____
              Signature _____

Mail, fax, phone, or e-mail your order to:

Glossbrenner's Choice   215-736-1213 (voice)
699 River Road   215-736-1031 (fax)
Yardley, PA 19067-1965   **alfred@delphi.com**
                                   70065.745@compuserve.com

Index

I HATE THAT WORD —"ONLINE."

E

EarthLink Network, 31
EDGAR, 185
education, elementary and secondary, 141–142
Educorp, 64
Election Line, 160
electronic mail. *See* e-mail
Electronic Zoo, 188–189
elementary education, 141–142
e-mail, 12–13, 42
    addresses, 44, 62
    advantages of using, 60–61
    browser program settings, 207–208
    cost considerations, 61
    message size, 65
    privacy, 64
    sending binary files, 62–65
    sending plain text files, 64–65
    software considerations, 27–28
    using Netscape for, 222–223
encryption, 64
Encryption Tools disk, 233
Epicurious, 164
error-checking protocol, 63–64
ESPNET Sports Zone, 191
Eudora, 27, 222
European Lab for Particle Physics, 14
Excite, 93, 99
Exec-PC, 150
external modems, 17–18

F

false drops, 96–97
FAQs, 66, 107, 232
Favorite Places, 56, 57, 215–217
fax modems, 18
fax software, 19
Federal Web Locator, 156
Feldman, Michael, 7
file compression, 80–82
files
    getting via FTP, 82–85
    naming conventions, 80
    saving, 57, 218–219
    self-extracting, 82
    types of, 79–80

File Transfer Protocol. *See* FTP (File Transfer Protocol)
films, 178–179
finance, personal, 4–5, 181–185
financial aid, 143
Fine Art Forum Mailing List, 128
Finger, 44
flaming, 42, 69
Foamation, 7
folders, file, 83
fonts, 52
food, 164
Forums, 22
Foxfire books, 106
frames, 214
free software, 43, 145–150
free-text search, 96
free trial offers, 21, 32
freeware, 145, 147
Frequently Asked Questions. *See* FAQs
FTP Essentials disk, 231–232
FTP (File Transfer Protocol), 54
    defined, 43
    getting files with, 82–85
    list of sites, 116–117
full text, advantages of, 131
full-text search, 96

G

Game Page of the Universe, 153–154
games, 151–154
Games Domain, 154
gardening, 162
Global Network Navigator (GNN), 30, 194
Glossbrenner's Choice, 34, 233–235
GNN Personal Finance Center, 181–182
GNN Travel Page, 194–195
GolfWeb, 192–193
Gopher, 54
    America Online's, 77–78
    defined, 43
    example of, 76–77
    finding sites, 78
    history of, 75
    menu creation, 75
    searching with, 101–103
Gopherspace, 95
Gourmet, 164

government information, 5–6, 155–160
graphic images, saving, 57, 219
Graphic Workshop, 80, 233
Gross, Terry, 121–122
GUNZIP, 85

H

Hahn, Harley, 77
hardware problems, 135–139
hardware requirements, 16–18
Hart, Michael, 131
Hayes modems, 17
helper applications, 53, 209–210
Hepburn, Katharine, 10
high-speed connections, 35
Hillside Elementary School, 141–142
hitchhiking, 6–7
homework, 6
HotJava, 211
hot links, 15, 53
Hotlist, 56
HotSpots, 215–217
HTML (HyperText Markup Language),
    52–53, 57, 218, 219
hub-and-spoke networks, 10
Hubble Space Telescope, 186–187
Huckleberry Finn, 84–85
humor, 166–169
hypertext, 15, 53
HyperText Markup Language. See HTML
    (HyperText Markup Language)

I

InfoMac, 64
Infoseek, 93, 94, 95–98
Integrated Services Digital Network
    (ISDN), 35
interest rates, credit card, 183
internal modems, 17–18
International Data Corporation (IDC), 66
Internet
    accuracy of information on, 94
    contrasted with Big Three consumer
        systems, 40
    contrasted with hub-and-spoke
        networks, 10–11
    cost considerations, 20–21, 25–27, 35

defined, 9
features, 11–12, 41–43, 44, 66
free resource lists, 111–117
gaining access, 12, 20–21, 25, 26, 29–31
getting connected, 25–26
history of, 9–12, 14–15
hype, 4
impact on daily life, 4, 8
informal rules, 42
search tools
    Gopher, 101–103
    search engines, 93–100
    Veronica, 103–105
Internet Basics disk, 232
Internet Book Information Center (IBIC), 133
Internet Computer Index, 139
Internet Explorer, 200
Internet Relay Chat (IRC), 44
Internet Service Provider (ISP), 20
    cost considerations, 25–26, 35
    customer support, 28
    how to find and select, 34–36
    list, 34
    locating via newsgroups, 35
    nationwide offerings, 31
    ten questions to ask, 36
Internet Slick Tricks, 41
Internet Toolkit, 34, 230–233
Internet Yellow Pages, The, 77, 78, 115
investing, 181–185
IRC (Internet Relay Chat), 44
IRS tax forms, 158
ISDN (Integrated Services Digital
    Network), 35
ISP. See Internet Service Provider (ISP)

J

Java, 211–212
Jefferson, Thomas, 158
jobs, 170–173
jokes, 166–169
Jughead, 103, 104
Jumbo!, 150
Just the FAQs disk, 232

K

Kantrowitz, Mark, 143
Kemp, Jack, 5
Kennedy, Joyce Lain, 173

kilobits per second (Kbps), 19
Koblas Currency Converter, 196

L

landscaping, 162
laptop computers, 17
Late Show with David Letterman, The, 168
Lava Computer Manufacturing, 18
Lawrence, David C., 107
Lawrence List, 107–108, 227, 232–233
legislation, 158
Letterman, David, 168
Library of Congress, 14, 87–89, 134, 158
Lipper Mutual Fund Scorecard, 5
Little Online Book, The, 57
Lycos, 93
.LZH files, 82

M

MacCompress, 85
Macintosh file compression tools, 81–82
Macintosh shareware, 148, 150
MacUser shareware awards, 148
Mad About You, 179–180
Magellan, 99
mail. *See* e-mail
Mail and News Preferences, 207–208
Mailing List Essentials disk, 232
mailing lists, 42–43
    contrasted with newsgroups, 70
    getting lists of, 71–72
    history of, 71
    sample descriptions, 73
    subscribing to, 72
mainframe computers, 9–10
MCI, 26
medical information, 174–176
memory cache, 205
menu systems, 43
message threads, 69
Microsoft, 200, 211
Microsoft Network (MSN), 20, 24, 31
    toll-free number, 24
MIT, 132, 184
Moby Dick, 14
modems
    how to buy, 17
    internal *vs.* external, 17–18

leading manufacturers, 17
    speed of, 18, 19
MOO (Multi-User Dungeon Object-
    Oriented), 44
Mosaic, 15, 200
Movie Database, 178–179
movie reviews, 178
Mozilla, 200
MPEG, 209
MUD (Multi-User Dungeon), 44
multimedia, 47–48, 209–210
multiple sessions, 220
MUSE (Multi-User Shared Environment), 44
MUSH (Multi-User Shared Hallucination), 44
mutual funds, 5
Myst, 151–153

N

National Air and Space Museum, 189
National Center for Supercomputing
    Applications (NCSA), 15
national Internet Service Providers, 31
NCSA, 15
Net, 4. *See also* Internet
Netcom Online Communication Services, 31
Netiquette, 66, 69
NetLauncher, 202
Net news, 42, 66–67. *See also* newsgroups
Netscape, 15, 200. *See also* browser programs
    e-mail features, 222–223
    home page, 93
    online help, 221
    reading newsgroups with, 224–226
Netscape Chat, 210
Netscape Communications, 15
Netscape Handbook, 201
Netscape Navigator, 15, 200. *See also*
    Netscape
Netscape Power Pack, 210
Netscape SmartMarks, 215
Netscape User Groups, 221
newbies
    advice for, 55
    defined, 21
    recommendations for, 23, 32
news.announce.newgroups, 108
news.announce.newusers, 107
news.answers, 107, 108

U

U16, 85
UART, 18
Ultimate TV List, 179
Uniform Resource Locator (URL), 48, 54–55
University of Michigan, 112
University of Minnesota, 75
University of North Carolina, 67
URL (Uniform Resource Locator), 48, 54–55
USA Today sports scores, 191
Usenet, 42, 67. *See also* newsgroups
USENIX, 67
US Robotics modems, 17
UU-CODE, 64, 65, 231

V

V.34, 18, 19
verifying documents, 206
Veronica, 103–105
Virtual Hospital, 175–176
Virtual Shareware Library, 150
viruses, 149
voice mail, 19
VT-100, 89

W

Wall Street Journal, 4–5
Web, 4. *See also* World Wide Web
Web Browser Cookbook
  how to use the, 55–56
Web browser programs. *See* browser
  programs; Mosaic; Netscape
WebCompass, 99–100
WebCrawler, 93
Web66 International WWW Schools
  Registry, 141
Weblinks travel information, 195
WebMuseum Network, 126–129
Whad'ya Know, 7
White House, 159–160

Whois, 44
WHYY, 6
Wilsonline CD-ROM, 6
WinCIM, 33, 202
Windows/DOS shareware, 149, 150
Windows file compression tools, 81–82
Windows Shareware Archive, 150
WINSOCK.DLL, 202
World Art Treasures, 129
WorldNet, AT&T's, 29–30
World Wide Web
  accessing via the Big Three, 48
  case-sensitivity of addresses, 48, 55
  defined, 9, 42
  history of, 14–15
  hype, 4
  impact on daily life, 4, 8
  publishing on the, 5–6
World Wide Web Essentials disk, 231
WOW!, 30, 32
Wright Brothers, 189

Y

Yahoo!, 93, 98–99
  games directory, 153
  jokes and humor directory, 167–168
YaleInfo Gopher, 78
Yanoff, Scott, 115
Yanoff List, 78, 86, 115–116, 232

Z

ZD Net, 148
.Z files, 85
Ziff-Davis, 139
Zimmerman, Frederick, 133
Zimmermann, Philip, 64
zip codes, 157
.ZIP files, 82
Zoom modems, 17

Order Form

USA 800–283–9444 ■ 510–548–4393 ■ FAX 510–548–5991
CANADA 800–387–8028 ■ 416–447–1779 ■ FAX 800–456–0536 OR 416–443–0948

Qty	Title	Price	Total

SUBTOTAL	
ADD APPLICABLE SALES TAX*	
SHIPPING	
TOTAL	

Shipping is by UPS ground: $4 for first item, $1 each add'l.
*We are required to pay sales tax in all states with the exceptions of AK, DE, HI, MT, NH, NV, OK, OR, SC and WY. Please include appropriate sales tax if you live in any state not mentioned above.

Customer Information

NAME

COMPANY

STREET ADDRESS

CITY   STATE   ZIP

PHONE (   )   FAX (   )
[REQUIRED FOR CREDIT CARD ORDERS]

Payment Method

❏ CHECK ENCLOSED   ❏ VISA   ❏ MASTERCARD   ❏ AMEX

CREDIT CARD #   EXP. DATE

COMPANY PURCHASE ORDER #

Tell Us What You Think

PLEASE TELL US WHAT YOU THOUGHT OF THIS BOOK: TITLE:_____

WHAT OTHER BOOKS WOULD YOU LIKE US TO PUBLISH?

PEACHPIT PRESS ■ 2414 Sixth Street ■ Berkeley, CA 94710

More from Peachpit Press

Gay and Lesbian Online

Jeff Dawson

In this gay-specific guide to the online world, author Jeff Dawson takes you on a thoroughly entertaining tour of the entire online terrain of gay and lesbian interests. Topics include those narrowly tied to gay culture, such as dating, adoptions, legal issues, clubs, and organizations, to more general areas such as travel, personal finance, health, and music. Sites of interest can be reached through the World Wide Web, America Online, CompuServe, and BBSs coast to coast. $19.95 (*200 pages*)

Head for the Web: Your Windows Connection to the World Wide Web

Mary Jane Mara

Head for the Web provides you with all you need to tap the World Wide Web, from browsing to HTML coding to setting up a Web server. The book includes in-depth tours of the three leading Windows-based browsers: Netscape, Mosaic, and Microsoft Network's Internet Explorer. The accompanying CD-ROM contains Netscape 2.0 (for Windows 3.1 and Windows 95) and an easy-to-use program that gives you dial-up access to the Web via Earthlink, a national Internet service provider. Covers both Windows 3.1 and Windows 95. $24.95 (*272 pages*)

HTML for the World Wide Web: Visual QuickStart Guide

Elizabeth Castro

This book is a step-by-step guide on using Hypertext Markup Language to design pages for the World Wide Web. The book presumes no prior knowledge of HTML or even the Internet, and uses clean, concise instructions. From titles, headers and logos to complex tables and clickable graphics, this book covers it all. Because of its well-organized format, it also serves as a day-to-day reference for experienced Web designers. Contains all the Hypertext Markup Language codes you need to create great Web pages. $17.95 (*176 pages*)

The Little PC Book, 2nd Edition: A Gentle Introduction to Personal Computers

Lawrence J. Magid with Kay Yarborough Nelson

Wouldn't you love having a knowledgeable, witty, endlessly patient pal to coach you through buying and using a PC? Well, you do. Popular columnist and broadcaster Larry Magid's expertise is yours in *The Little PC Book*, described by *The Wall Street Journal* as "the class of the field." This edition includes the latest on Windows 95, the Internet, CD-ROMs, and more. Includes a handy Windows 95 Cookbook section. $18.95 (*384 pages*)

The Little Online Book

Alfred Glossbrenner

This beginner's guide gives you everything you need to begin exploring the electronic universe from your desktop. You can correspond with people all over the world, look up information, shop, join electronic clubs, download free software, and more with the help of this friendly, nontechnical book. Covers modems, communication software, the Internet, commercial online services, bulletin boards, and many other topics. Includes a step-by-step cookbook explaining common online tasks. $17.95 *(426 pages)*

NETSCAPE 2 for Macintosh: Visual QuickStart Guide

Elizabeth Castro

NETSCAPE 2 for Windows: Visual QuickStart Guide

Elizabeth Castro

More than 75 percent of all people browsing the World Wide Web use Netscape, in part because of the program's many powerful features. Using the *Visual QuickStart Guide* series' proven rich graphical approach, the book helps readers go from installing the software to using its advanced capabilities, and fully explains all the features of the 2.0 version of Netscape. The browser's advances include a built-in emailer, support for reading newsgroups, a much-improved bookmark editor, support for superscript and subscript text, and a new plug-in architecture that allows seamless integration of Quicktime movies, Adobe Acrobat PDF documents, and Director multimedia presentations right into Web pages. $16.95 *(200 pages)*

PageMill for Macintosh: Visual QuickStart Guide

Maria Langer

Learn how to create Web pages the fast and fun way with PageMill, the red-hot Web authoring tool from Adobe. PageMill offers an easy-to-use way for non-technical users to create Web pages without knowing HTML coding. By taking away all the scary technical details, PageMill allows users to focus on content and design. In no time at all, readers will be designing and creating Web pages. *PageMill for Macintosh: Visual QuickStart Guide* is packed with hundreds of screenshots, plus clear instructions and loads of helpful tips, to guide readers through basic editing techniques, applying styles, working with graphic images and links, and finally, to testing and enhancing their new Web pages. $15.95 *(160 pages)*

What's on the Internet, Third Edition

Eric Gagnon

This "TV Guide" for the Internet is an informative, fun, and useful way to find out what online discussion and information groups exist on the Internet and how to connect with them. The book features mini-reviews of 2,300 of the most popular newsgroups, some 21,000 Frequently Asked Questions (FAQ) files, a 5,500-word alphabetically organized subject index, and a list of more than 8,000 Internet newsgroups. For the third edition, all reviews have been updated, the section on business applications on the Internet has been greatly expanded, and there are dozens of new images. It's the easiest, fastest way to find a particular topic on the Internet, and is the only book that focuses on newsgroups, the core of the Internet. For new and experienced Internet users $24.95 *(400 pages, available June '96)*

Five Free Days...
to check out the Web with EarthLink Network's TotalAccess™ and Netscape Navigator™ 2.0!

Your All-In-One Web Connection

Send in the attached coupon and receive five free days to surf the Web with EarthLink Network's TotalAccess™ and Netscape Navigator™ 2.0.

What's included with the EarthLink diskettes:

- EarthLink Network Registration—your point-and-click guide to getting hooked to the Web in about 10 minutes
- Internet Dialer—connects your modem to the Internet at up to 28,800 bps
- Netscape Navigator™ 2.0 not only lets you browse the Web, but also includes new powerful e-mail and news-group features. And it handles audio, video, and animation plug-ins to fully exploit the Web's multimedia powers.

Surf free for five days after you first register. After that, you can cancel the service without further obligation or keep on surfing with Earthlink. EarthLink's TotalAccess service costs $19.95 a month for unlimited service, plus a $25 one-time setup fee. Netscape 2.0—worth $49 alone—is bundled into the EarthLink Network TotalAccess™ package and can only be used with EarthLink. Ongoing TotalAccess service includes 2 megabytes of space on Earthlink's server for your own Web home page.

- -

Please send me my copy of the EarthLink Network TotalAccess™ diskette package with Internet Dialer and Netscape Navigator™ 2.0 and five free days worth of connect time.

Your name _____

Street _____

City _____ State _____ Zip _____

Phone number _____

Which computer operating system are you using?

☐ Macintosh   ☐ Windows 3.1   ☐ Windows 95

Send to:

EarthLink Network • 3100 New York Drive • Pasadena, CA 91107

EarthLink Network™

PEACHPIT PRESS

The Little Web Book